WILLIAM PFAFF

Civilization and the

The
WRATH
of
NATIONS

Furies of Nationalism

SIMON & SCHUSTER

New York • London • Toronto • Sydney • Tokyo • Singapore

SIMON & SCHUSTER
Simon & Schuster Building
Rockefeller Center
1230 Avenue of the Americas
New York, New York 10020

Library of Congress Cataloging-in-Publication Data

Pfaff, William, date.
   The wrath of nations : civilization and the furies of nationalism
/ William Pfaff.
      p.   cm.
   Includes bibliographical references and index.
   1. Nationalism. 2. Violence. 3. World politics. I. Title
JC311.P436   1993
320.5'4—dc20   93-26058   CIP
ISBN: 0-671-72829-6

TO C., A., AND N.

Home is where one starts from. As we grow older
The world becomes stranger, the pattern more complicated
. . . Not the intense moment
Isolated, with no before and after,
But a lifetime burning in every moment . . .

Contents

And when you hear of wars and revolts, do not be alarmed by it; such things must happen, but the end is not so soon. . . . Nation will rise in arms against nation, and kingdom against kingdom; there will be great earthquakes in this region or that, and plagues and famines; and sights of terror and great portents from heaven.

—Luke 21:9–12

Les Morts gouvernent les Vivants.

—Auguste Comte

1 *Nationalism*

This book is about the most powerful political force of the twentieth century, which is likely to prove the most powerful of the twenty-first as well: nationalism. Nationalism is a profound, if often malign, expression of human identities, a negative force, but also a positive one. It is an expression of love as well as of hate. It is a fundamental element in modern political life and international relations. It demands to be better understood.

The book describes where nationalism comes from, why, and when, and estimates where it is taking us. It considers the historical sources of nationalism, and also its counterparts and counterfeits in the evolution of modern society, not only in Western Europe, where the nation-state originated and is dominant, and in America, but in Asia and Africa as well, where western ideas of nationalism, as of internationalism, have exerted decisive, and frequently destructive, influence during recent years.

Nationalism has been the cause of much hateful violence in modern history, and is so again today in the Balkans and the states of the former Soviet Union. The related phenom-

14   ena of communal and racial violence afflict parts of Asia and
Africa. However, nationalism is also the force which con-
founded and broke the imperialism of Lenin's heirs, and
Nazism's domination of Europe in the 1940s. The two totalitarian internationalist movements of this century have crimes
to their account much worse than any of the crimes yet produced by nationalism, horrifying as the latter are.

Nationalism is usually thought a primordial historical
phenomenon, the emotional binding by which political communities originally emerged, and through which the ethnic
community finds its historical expression and maturity. It
also is usually taken to be an essential but passing stage in the
march of history, necessary in producing the modern nation,
but also to be left behind as more rational and progressive
forms of political society take the place of the more backward.

This is not true. Nationalism is a phenomenon of the
European nineteenth century. It is a political consequence of
the literary-intellectual movement called Romanticism, a
Central European reaction to the universalizing, and there-
fore disorienting, ideas of the eighteenth-century French
Enlightenment.

Nationalism is not an ideology because it has no universality. It is impossible to be a nationalist as such, only a
German or Croatian or American nationalist. However,
nationalism occupies the moral and emotional ground otherwise held by political ideology. It is unreasonable, considered
as a general phenomenon, while natural as a specific one. It is
contradictory as well as preposterous as a general proposition that the values and interests of every country are superior ones, yet it is evident that all nations are the same as

objects of the loyalty of their citizens. Only a Serb can appre-
ciate why Serbia is worth dying for, since Serbia otherwise
represents nothing of more value or moment to the detached
observer than does Croatia, or Guatemala, or Tibet.

The nation-state itself is modern. The number of nations with a more or less coherent history of independent
existence before modern times is fairly small: England
(Britain), Japan, France, Denmark (but not in its present
borders), Sweden, Russia (Muscovy), Poland, Spain and Portugal. . . . Even here there is doubt. France, for example, existed as a kingdom, an empire—a revolution; but it has been
argued that there was no French nation until Jules Ferry established universal free education in the nineteenth century.
The emergence of a Russian nation, subsequently an empire, based on Muscovy's ascendance over the Tatars of the
Golden Horde, took place only in the eighteenth and nineteenth centuries. Spain even today experiences Catalan as
well as Basque separatism.

Germany's unification, under Prussia, occurred only in
1871; its reunification, without most of Prussia, in 1990. Austria-Hungary was never a nation, but an empire. Austria itself became a nation in 1918, but the Austrians willingly gave
up their nation when Hitler launched the *Anschluss* in 1938.
The Roman empire was Italian, but Italy did not exist until
the mid-nineteenth century. Lombardy, the kingdom of
Sicily, the kingdom of Naples, the Venetian Empire, the Pa-
pal States, Savoy and Piedmont—they are what existed before. Greece vanished into the Roman Empire before the
birth of Christ and reemerged from the Ottoman Empire
only in the nineteenth century.

Outside Europe, there have been no nations other than
those, among them the United States, which were estab-

16 lished as Europe's outposts. Japan is the serious exception to that generalization. Siam and Cambodia, like China, were kingdoms, realms, not nations with corporate consciousnesses. India was a Hindu civilization dominated—after the Moghuls came—by an Islamic elite, and, after that, by a British one.

France and England were the original nation-states, and their history as nations dates from the Hundred Years' War (1337–1453). Most of the other European nations, as such, originated in the eighteenth or nineteenth centuries. The United States is an older nation than Germany or Italy. The original form of human political organization was the agricultural or hunting community, leading to the city, the religious civilization with a god-king, and the dynastic realm or empire of expanding and inclusive borders. The Dutch Republic (1652–1672) was the first non-dynastic, non-city state. The modern nation, a European phenomenon, arrived when the empires declined, and that happened quite recently.

The ethnic nation is an invention, also a modern one. Of the major contemporary nation-states, none can seriously claim to be, or to have ever been, ethnically homogeneous, except for Japan (yet Japan has its aboriginal population), Finland, possibly the Scandinavian states (but there are four of them, so they are not exclusive), Albania, and possibly Hungary (but what is historical Hungary without its Jews?).

There has been no "natural" evolution from the primitive community, ethnic or otherwise, to the nation. There is no discernible general progressive movement towards international community, even though the twentieth century has seen five major formal attempts to create a new international system (six, if we include the Japanese effort to establish an

Asian "coprosperity sphere"). Two were totalitarian, repressive, and genocidal. Three have been liberal and voluntarist, of which one, the League of Nations, ignominiously failed; a second, the United Nations, is considerably less of a success than its creators intended; and the last, the European Community, has been a great success until recently, but in 1992 and 1993 fell into grave confusion. The Greek, Roman, feudal Christian, Hapsburg, and Ottoman periods in the past were all more internationalist, cosmopolitan, polyglot, and inclusive than international society has been since 1918.

Nationalism, of course, is intrinsically absurd. Why should the accident—fortune or misfortune—of birth as an American, Albanian, Scot, or Fiji Islander impose loyalties that dominate an individual life and structure a society so as to place it in formal conflict with others? In the past there were local loyalties to place and clan or tribe, obligations to lord or landlord, dynastic or territorial wars, but primary loyalties were to religion, God or god-king, possibly to emperor, to a civilization as such. There was no nation.

To be Chinese was to belong to a civilization which was presumed to be universal, or, if not universal, to have only barbarians beyond it. To be Mesopotamian or Roman was to belong to an inclusive empire of undetermined borders. The foreigner fortunate enough to be incorporated into Rome's empire sought the privilege of citizenship: to be able to say, "*Civis Romanus sum.*" Rome was not a nation; it was a city and empire both.

To be a European in the Middle Ages was, for the vast majority, to be a Christian, with obligations and rights with respect to a landholding hierarchy dependent, in theory at least, upon the Christian emperor, the Roman emperor's

18   successor, and the pope, God's vicar on earth. One might fight against a liege lord's rival, or the emperor's enemies, or go on crusade against the pagans or heretics, but there still was no nation, and no nationalism in the modern sense of that term. None of these obligations to war was connected to membership in a distinct and individual ethnic group or political entity different from all others.

The language communities which later coincided with some nations (not all) were still in formation. The magnificent sixteenth-century flowering of English literature was a celebration of the invention of the language, freshly emerged from Saxon dialects and Norman French. The latter was itself, like the Southern European languages, in continuing development from Latin. It is argued that France did not speak French until the nineteenth century.

There are dialects everywhere in Europe even today which are incomprehensible, or virtually so, to the majority of speakers, preserving elements of other languages, and of the past of the majority language. Appalachian English in the United States preserved marked Elizabethan elements as late as the 1950s. I knew young men and women in the South then who "frolicked" on Saturday nights (a word from the Dutch, incidentally, not Old English), and who would declare that a place lay in "yon" direction. Gullah then, in the Carolina coastlands, preserved West African linguistic structures, and continues to do so even today.

Languages die. I have heard an Estonian poet express the fear that after the inroads made during fifty years of a totalitarian "red language" into the existing "white language" of her country, words such as *freedom* and *peace* and *democracy* have been "stolen," and refined forms of expression lost, having been forbidden, so that the language itself is greatly di-

20 tion), Poles, Italians, Spaniards, Portuguese, Armenians (particularly after the First World War, when immigration was encouraged in order to rebuild after the huge loss in male population). Still more recent arrivals are Indochinese, Lebanese, Algerians (Moslems, Jews, and also the so-called *pieds-noirs*, former French Algerian settlers of nineteenth-century Mediterranean European origin), Moroccans, Tunisians, and Africans from France's former sub-Saharan colonies. The latter groups are objects of controversy and discrimination but have been given citizenship in large numbers, and are a highly visible presence.* The only possible answers to the question of what it is to be a Frenchman today are cultural and political. French nationhood, like Britain's, is historical and cultural, not ethnic, even though there are physical types which one readily thinks of as "typically" French, or British (or German or Dutch or Spanish).

Spain is Iberian, Celtic, Visigoth, Vandal, Phoenician, Greek—and Catalan, Castilian, Basque, and Arab. Portugal is African as well as Lusitanian, Celt, and Visigoth (German). Even isolated Ireland—Christianity's North Atlantic refuge after Rome's fall—had its Norse invaders and has its "black" Irish, dark haired and dark eyed, offspring, so the story has it, of Spaniards shipwrecked from the Armada. The United States, of course, is now the least ethnic of all nations (although one of the most nationalistic), since it has been by

---

*The tennis star Yannick Noah is half Cameroonian; the film star Isabelle Adjani half Algerian; the late singer and actor Yves Montand Italian. Albert Camus was a half-Spanish *pied-noir* Algerian. The eminent contemporary novelist Julian Green, a member of the French Academy, is even an American, of an unrepentant expatriate Confederate family from Savannah. Edouard Balladur, named prime minister of France in 1993, was born in Izmir, son of a Levantine Christian family possessing French nationality, which had come to Turkey from what now is Azerbaijan two centuries earlier, and which settled in France only in 1935.

minished and might not recover, even though the constraints   *19*
now are abolished. There are, she felt, too few to restore Estonian. But would Estonia die if Estonian proved irrecoverable? National feeling has survived in Scotland, Ireland, and Wales long after the Celtic languages disappeared from the ordinary discourse of the overwhelming majority. Only a conscious effort preserves Breton and Basque. Provençal has disappeared, but Provence survives.

The original nations were created by dynastic hazard, and had no unitary ethnic base. England's prehistoric population suffered invasion by the Celts and Danes before the Roman conquest, and by various Germanic peoples afterwards, coming under Norman French (which is to say Scandinavian) rule and colonization in 1066. Since 1945 Britain has acquired Indian, Pakistani, Bangladeshi, and West Indian minorities (African and Indo-Pakistani in origin), a recolonization of the colonizer by the colonized—a phenomenon experienced by some of the other former European colonial powers as well. Even Britain's monarchy is German, before that was Dutch, and before that was Scottish. There has been no "English" king since the eleventh century.

France incorporates Vikings, Belgians, Germans, the Gauls of Caesar's wars, Bretons (Celts), Catalans, Basques, and Latin Provençals (speakers of the *langue d'oc*) as well as survivors from its prehistoric population. The wars with England brought Scots and Irish to France ("the wild geese"), who stayed, their names figuring incongruously among the French aristocracy of today.

In more recent times there have been Jews (France was second to the United States as the object of nineteenth- and early-twentieth-century Russian and Polish Jewish migra-

design the assimilator of immigrant populations from all over the world, with American nationalism a force of assimilation and acculturation (objectives today, of course, repudiated by many Americans). In a more qualified way this also is true of the immigrant nations of the old "white Commonwealth"—Canada, Australia, New Zealand, and white South Africa.

In contrast, in East-Central and Balkan Europe nationality is identified with ethnic or religious identity. It is not acquired by immigration (nor readily lost by emigration). This makes a radical difference, and is at the source of the crises of nationalism which have broken out in the region since the collapse of Communism in 1989. Nationality is perceived as detached from territory, although certain territories may be held essential to nations, as Serbs insist with respect to regions they have conquered from Croatia and Bosnia-Herzegovina, and also to the Serbian province of Kosovo: that its medieval importance to Serbia makes it forever Serb, even though Kosovo has since become all but totally populated by Moslem Albanians. Transylvania is held by Romanians to be integral to Romania even though its population is largely Hungarian. There are many such cases.

Poland existed for 123 years in the absence of a territory recognized to be Poland. Between 1918, when it resumed territorial existence after its eighteenth-century partitions (when it entirely disappeared into Prussia, Russia, and Austria), and the present day, Poland's boundaries have shifted westward by more than 150 miles on its eastern frontier and some 70 in the west (in a country before the war only 500 miles wide). Part of what formerly was Poland now is in Lithuania and Ukraine, including the great cultural centers

22 of Wilno (Vilnius) and Lwow (Lvov, Lemberg); and part of today's Poland was formerly Prussia. Adam Zamoyski writes that as a result of the Second World War "Poland's frontiers were wrenched back to an idealized original; the minorities which had not been extirpated were removed; Poles from all over Eastern Europe were concentrated. The loss of Wilno and Lwow, and the disappearance of the Jewish, Ruthene and German elements, have impoverished the cultural variety of the Polish world. The compensatory factors are political rather than cultural." It would be presumptuous to think that Poland's territorial definition may not change again.

During its years of territorial non-existence the Polish nation survived in the minds of Poles living both in what had been historical Poland and in exile in Paris and elsewhere. When for the second time it ceased to possess an independent national existence, during the Second World War, underground schools were created, as during the Partition years, as were universities (called "flying" universities because their clandestine classes were held in constantly changing places) and even underground institutions of civil administration and justice, in order to assert a Polish nation's political existence despite its formal non-existence. When Lech Walesa became president of the reconstituted non-Communist Polish Republic in 1990, he accepted the insignia of office not from General Jaruzelski, his predecessor as president of the Polish People's Republic, but from the elderly chief of state of the Polish government in exile, which was installed in Paris and moved to London in 1941.

During the years of exile, Poles working in London with the wartime allies, or serving in Polish ships, army brigades, and air squadrons attached to British forces, and later—after the Soviet Union had installed the Communist party in power in Poland—those Poles who worked in New York, London, or Munich with the western intelligence agencies and western-sponsored radio stations broadcasting to Poland, conducted themselves as agents of a nation temporarily denied its freedom, but in principle the equal of the American or British nations with which they cooperated and upon which events had made them temporarily, and reluctantly, dependent. They attempted to maintain the principle of a relationship of reciprocity between allied powers, their own temporarily embarrassed by fortune, but able eventually to make good its obligations. It was, to those Americans and British who worked with these Poles, an edifying performance. It contrasted, in the 1950s, with the attitude of many others from Soviet-controlled nations in the East who worked with western governments, and certainly wanted to see their countries freed, but who saw themselves as émigrés and expected to install their families and children in the West for good.

The modern western nation is a practical affair. It provides defense, civil order, a system of justice, an economic structure, a framework for industry and for commercial transactions, systems of transportation and communications, and so on. It demands solidarity among its citizens, which means their willingness to accept the moral and legal norms of the collectivity, to pay taxes and otherwise support the government apparatus from which all benefit, and to come to the common defense. Citizenship is a matter of obligations and reciprocal benefits, although it nearly always has an emotional coloration as well, often intense—an at-

24   tachment to country, *patrie*, or "fatherland" that repeatedly
has caused people to disregard others' claims to justice, or
disregard reason, or a common morality.

This national feeling, which is not a practical commitment but a matter of passions, has consistently overridden
principles of international solidarity and political or religious universalism. The first Socialist International cracked
up in 1914 when members of the international working class
enthusiastically went to war with one another for purely nationalistic reasons. Christians and Jews have rarely hesitated
to serve in the armies of nations at war with one another,
whatever the cause. The European colonial powers successfully employed Moslem troops against fellow Moslems,
Hindus against Hindus, African troops to keep order in
mutinous African colonies, and so on.

However, this emotional attachment is not essential to a
nation. It is argued that there was no Belgian nation at all until the First World War, when the shock of German invasion
produced intense and unexpected resistance from both fran-
cophone and Dutch-speaking Belgians. The Belgian nation
nonetheless exacts a very low emotional commitment from
the majority of its citizens, for a number of historical reasons,
which include long foreign occupation, with a consequent
role for government as agent of foreign interests, and the ac-
rimonious coexistence inside the country of French and
Dutch linguistic communities. The function of the central
government is reduced to absolute minimum in new constitu-
tional arrangements put forward in 1993. Many of the functions of the central government have already been devolved
upon the Walloon, Flemish, and (binational) Brussels authorities. Many Belgians would willingly reassign the rest to
"Europe," with Brussels becoming an internationalized city.

Yet the argument that Belgium is merely a nineteenth-century political artifice, convenient at the time to Prussia, Britain, and France, must address the fact that surveys of the value attitudes of the Walloons and Flemish show that the two have more in common with one another than the Walloons do with the French or the Flemish with the Dutch. There *is* a Belgian nation, created by the common historical experience of Catholics in this flat and much-fought-over seaboard land where French and Dutch-Germanic cultures meet.

Canada bears a certain resemblance to Belgium. The majority of modern Canadians seem never to have satisfactorily settled in their minds why there should be a Canada. The nation exists as the result of the Seven Years' War and that war's aftermath in Europe, the rebellion against the British crown of the other thirteen of Britain's North American colonies—and the Battle of Vimy Ridge in the First World War, in which Canadians first fought as Canadians and not as citizens of individual provinces. But it sometimes seems that citizens of the United States believe more in Canada's necessity (as a non–United States America: evidence of alternative possibility, demonstration of non-inevitability—even refuge) than do Canadians themselves. Quebec is a nation. But it is unclear that English-speaking Canada really is—which seems a pity.

Modern Germany, since the Second World War, presents the case of a people (German, but also Slav, Baltic, Dutch, French) deeply conscious of themselves as a political and historical entity, who in recent history have defined citizenship by "blood," unlike their West European neighbors, yet who nonetheless, like the Belgians, but for different rea-

26   sons, have also wished to unload as much as possible of the responsibilities and apparatus of nationhood onto the supranational European Community. Modern German history has seemed to many Germans too painful to bear, so that a kind of resignation of independent statehood in favor of "Europe" has seemed to offer a definitive solution to their own "German problem." The secondary guilt that since the war has been part of being a German, the guilt of fathers visited, however unjustly, upon the sons and daughters, has seemed resolvable through Germany's absorption into a new Europe, free of guilt.

Yet this has been the reaction of people still, in the early 1990s, in a difficult situation, rather than solid evidence of a decline of German nationalism (a nationalism attached to a nation which was a single united nation only for seventy-nine years—until this resumed in 1990—and whose older, formative inheritance was that of feudal empire). It is imprudent to attempt final conclusions about the future of a Germany where most citizens, until 1990, considered both of the states they then possessed, the Federal Republic of Germany and the German Democratic Republic, provisional and incomplete entities, constructs of the war waiting to be replaced. The reunited Germany which did replace them might also be called provisional, since it has lost, and renounced, most of Prussia, the dynamic core of Bismarck's Germany.

German pride in West Germany's economic accomplishments has nonetheless been a form of nationalism, and has not lacked an edge of condescension with respect to those of Germany's allies who are its economic competitors and whose performance was less brilliant than that of the West German Federal Republic. On the other hand, since

1945 Germans have been consistently hostile to any German military role outside Germany. The pacific attitudes expressed in Germany during the Gulf War of 1991, and in the Yugoslav War, as during earlier Middle East crises, suggest that there may have been a permanent mutation in German political conviction and ambition, towards North European or Scandinavian-style neutralism or non-interventionism, replacing the aggressive nationalism which marked Germany's modern historical record until 1945. But this remains to be seen.

The salient quality of German "national" existence continues to be its inability to be a nation like the old nations of Western Europe. It has never been such a nation. It passed from feudalism to dynastic absolutism and empire in 1870, and, after the brief republican Weimar interval, to ideological totalitarianism after 1932. From the earliest feudal period the Germans of the Holy Roman Empire conceived themselves charged with a mission of conversion and colonization to the peoples to Germany's east. Under Adolf Hitler this became a secular and racialist mission to enslave or eliminate those peoples as racial inferiors. From the time that ended, in the Year Zero, 1945, until reunification in 1990, Germans seemed to want to renounce not only crusade and empire but nationhood itself, in order to abandon their history, closing the books on the past. Hence their distress in 1990 to find themselves rejoicing at the reconstitution of a united German nation—with a mission in the East.

The past cannot be left behind. Nations are the product of a history we are incapable of changing, or perhaps of forgiving. The twentieth century effectively began with the

28   First World War, the greatest of all wars of nationalism. The distress of Balkan and East-Central Europe as the twentieth century ends, like that of the Middle East, is the direct outcome of the destruction of the Hapsburg and Ottoman empires in 1918, and of how they were destroyed, leaving behind incoherent ethnic states. The Second World War began in the aggressions of internationalisms—Nazi, Leninist-Stalinist—and was settled by nationalism.* It was the direct and one may say inevitable product of the first war, the "Great" War, as (without inevitability) were Nazism itself, the Bolshevik Revolution and the reign of Leninism in Russia, and the upheaval subsequently produced by the admixture of Leninism with nationalism in Asia. The Great War was also responsible for the influence Leninism—and then Maoism—achieved in the West's own imagination and intelligence, a cautionary tale.

The United States' soaring national ascent, and descent, between 1900 and the century's end were the product of those two wars, and their cold war aftermath, which turned it from its rich private history, and conviction of private election as the Divinity's favorite, to an ideological internationalism and superpowerdom the country played out badly, with better results for others than for itself. The United States' ideological difference from other nations had exempted it from the crisis of national rivalries which produced the 1914 war—when, as Henry James had foreseen, from "the rottenness and extravagance" of then-contemporary society, "the Huns and Vandals will have to come up—from the black depths of . . . the enormous misery." So they did, taking bit-

*To characterize Nazism as an internationalist rather than nationalist movement is, I recognize, to go against the accepted opinion. I argue my case in Chapter 3.

ter joy in destruction, wrecking Europe as it then existed, and creating a new political universe which ended, in turn, in 1989.

But reconsider. In Asia the twentieth century might be said to have begun with the Russo-Japanese War of 1904–1905, a fatal blow to the czarist system in the one country, and sending the other nation towards an imperialism it proved incapable of sustaining in military terms, but has since 1945 reestablished commercially, to the disadvantage of the United States and of that Western Europe which ruled the world in 1904. The Japanese victory set nationalism loose in colonial Asia, confirming by Japan's own versatile and unnerving national success what other Asian peoples might do. The Japanese example was responsible for making Vietnam, Korea, and Thailand into modern nations, and had a great influence on the mammoth and murderous effort of the Chinese to make a modern nation out of China—an enterprise still to succeed.

Examine the evidence again: the century may be thought to have begun with the Spanish-American War of 1898, which ended Spain's five-hundred-year empire and great-power claims, and established the American Empire; or with the Boer War of 1899–1902, which began the moral collapse of Britain's empire and, by extension, of European imperialism itself, eventually bringing down Dutch, French, Belgian, and Portuguese empires. Each of these had been conceived as an international system as well as an extension of national power. With the exception of Britain and Belgium, all these imperial powers bitterly defended their empires when they came under nationalist (and liberal internationalist) pressures after the Second World War. The

30   Netherlands, France, and Portugal all fought wars (the Portuguese until 1974) to save their empires, and each failed. There undoubtedly would be no internationalist European Community today had they not failed and been compelled to abandon their notions of themselves as international societies. The American Empire was the last to fall, after defeat in an imperial war of its own, in Vietnam, which it did not understand to be what it really was.

The twentieth century has belonged to nationalism. Nationalism destroyed western imperialism and the colonial system, and also destroyed the ideological internationalisms which have been the distinctive political phenomena of the twentieth century, Leninism and Nazism. Nationalism has installed nations nearly everywhere. Of the some two hundred nations which now make up the United Nations, only a score or so, nearly all European or American, possessed national consciousness before 1914.

The technological and economic integration of modern international society, which has gone immensely far beyond what was imagined even in the 1950s and 1960s, coexists with national struggle of the most primitive kind among Serbs, Croats, Bosnians, and Kosovars in Southern Europe, otherwise members of the advanced industrial world; between Armenians and Azerbaijani; Moldavians and linguistic Russians; Ukrainians, Balts, and Russians; Arabs and Kurds and Jews; Persians and Arabs. It coexists with communal warfare involving Tamils and Sinhalese inside Sri Lanka; Sikhs and Hindus, and Hindus and Moslems, in India; Hutu and Tutsi and Twa in Central Africa; and, across the arc of sub-Saharan Africa, nomads and cultivators, Christians and Moslems, Moslems and animists—white and black.

The nationalism of the major powers has been displaced from war to commerce, but has not lost strength. Japan and the United States are no less ambitious and rival today than in 1941, but they grasp their mutual as well as competitive interests, and pursue them peacefully. The European powers have actually subordinated their individual nationalisms in a new consciousness of themselves as part of a European economic and political entity. However, a basic motive for this has been the conviction that such a transfer of "national" allegiance was essential for them to compete successfully with the United States (and, so it was thought, the U.S.S.R.); hence, European unification is an expression or instrument of nationalism as well as a subordination or sublimation of it. And West European unity has recently come under the shadow of doubt.

Nationalism was for many years thought a progressive cause, a modern movement of the popular interest against empire or dynasty, a struggle against privilege. "This was . . . the Jacobin view, derived from Rousseau. It was also going to be the view of liberals such as Giuseppe Mazzini . . . and John Stuart Mill," as Stanley Hoffman has said. It was the view accepted by Woodrow Wilson and the group of American intellectuals ("the Inquiry") which produced Wilson's 1918 peace proposals and committed the United States to the principle of universal national self-determination and the creation of a League of Nations (American membership in the latter was subsequently rejected by Congress). The Allies' partition of the Austro-Hungarian and Ottoman territories after 1918 on the basis of this principle actually left incoherent national states obsessed with their residual ethnic and national quarrels, contributing to the disorder culminat-

32   ing in the Second World War, a disorder which has broken out again since the collapse of the Soviet system in 1989–1990.

The argument before 1918 had been that the "reactionary" Hapsburg and Ottoman systems imprisoned "young" peoples meant by history to live individual national lives. This expressed the implicit assumptions of the Social Darwinism of the period: nations were young, vigorous, expanding; or mature and static; or in decline, ready to be displaced by others. The progressive reputation of European nationalism was lost in the interwar years, as parliaments faltered in the Balkans and Southeastern Europe, or were dismissed by monarchs or generals, and ethnic and national conflicts increasingly poisoned the political life of such countries as Austria, Yugoslavia, Czechoslovakia, Hungary, and Romania, inviting the Nazi interventions which followed.

The conduct of some of the newly established East European and Balkan nations also turned enlightened opinion against nationalism. The Scottish scholar and journalist who had been the principal West European advocate of a new South Slav state, R. W. Seton-Watson, wrote in despair, "I think they are both mad," as he witnessed the developing intolerance between Serbs and Croats in Yugoslavia in the 1930s. Western opinion now placed its faith in the new internationalism of the League of Nations, and after that in the United Nations organization, which was meant to be a reformed League, but was in turn thwarted by the Security Council veto and the cold war. Or progressives accepted the internationalist claims of the "socialism" of the Comintern and Soviet Union.

•

After the Second World War, progressive hopes were again attached to nationalism, with respect to the liberation of the Asian and African populations of the European colonial empires. It was generally held that granting them independence was a moral imperative upon the colonial powers, even if the new nations governed themselves badly (although it was the prevailing assumption that, freed of external restraint, they would govern themselves well; the influence of Rousseau's belief in the natural virtue of man—above all of "uncivilized," hence uncorrupted, man—was still powerful, as it remains even today). They mostly have governed themselves badly, but African and Asian nationalism remains a progressive cause, the tyrants it has produced generally granted, in western circles, until fairly recently, at least, an unstated exemption from the judgments on tyranny and human exploitation readily applied elsewhere.

In the aftermath of the great European liberations of 1989, to which the defiantly surviving nationalisms of the East European and Balkan countries had crucially contributed, nationalism once again regained its progressive reputation. Or so it was until the patriotism and nationalist conviction which previously had been directed against the Communist system, actually the agency of a Russian great-power nationalism, now were redirected to support the claims and grievances which each of the Balkan and Eastern European societies historically had harbored against those others with whom geography and politics had determined that it must live. Once again nationalism, "ethnic" or religious and historical in origin, undermined international peace, producing internecine war in what had been Yugoslavia, and in parts of the former Soviet Union, and threatening it elsewhere.

Romantic individualism produced the belief that the "unspoiled" and spontaneous were more authentic persons, and therefore closer to truth, than the intellectual or aristocratic. Their language was thought a purer expression of the primal feelings and knowledge of men. Old spoken languages accordingly were revived during the nineteenth century and provided with written forms and grammar, and folk poetry— thought closer to the innocent origins of man—was recorded. The political conclusion drawn was that submerged human communities with a common language should be recognized as political nations. Intellectuals developed written "literary" languages from the demotic or dialectical Greek, Macedonian, Slovak, Czech, Finnish, and Norwegian languages actually spoken by the peasant and worker populations of these "submerged" nations. The organization of political movements followed, devoted to national "renaissance" and recognition, sometimes fraudulent.* On the other hand, the Celtic revival in Ireland produced a revival of the language itself, and an explosion of poetry, fiction, and drama probably unmatched in an equivalent period anywhere—much of it, paradoxically enough, written in English rather than Irish, but inspired by Ireland's new sense of itself, and leading directly to the Irish political movement which produced the Easter Uprising of 1916 and the successful war against British domination which followed in 1919–1921.

As Talmon also says, Romanticism is an extreme expres-

---

*The British writer Neal Ascherson says: "The claim that modern Greece is a resurrection of the Greece—or rather Athens—in which democracy began is a concoction. It was dreamed up by patriots who lived in Bucharest or Paris, fervently encouraged by British Romantics in love with their own idea of Grecian purity and liberty. It is one of those feats of 'forging a nation' which nineteenth-century intellectuals performed so brilliantly."

sion of the belief that man is intrinsically good, and, unhindered, will find the best way to achieve the general interest. The practical consequences of this were often, and logically, unreasonable, including the cult of the genius and the artist who is absolved from the moral obligations of other mortals, and that of the man of action who assumes Faustian risks to overturn "bourgeois" morality and remake the world. The consequences of this kind of thinking shaped mid-twentieth-century European politics for the bitter worse.

The modern idea of political freedom is the product of Enlightenment philosophy itself, given practical form and an ideology in a revolution meant to free people from arbitrary power and to empower them as individuals. A qualitatively new knowledge seemed to exist as a result of the scientific discoveries of the eighteenth century. This knowledge seemed to offer the opportunity for a scientific reorganization of society, an enterprise which the French nation believed itself to have begun in the Revolution and continued under Napoleon. The French Revolution destroyed the absolutist monarchical system, which was supranational, on grounds that it was illogical. Bourbons, like Hapsburgs, were not national figures: they were dynastic families nominated by God or history to rule domains of unfixed frontiers, readily extended by marriage or war, or as easily diminished. The Revolution asserted individual rights, human individuality and worth, equality of individuals. In doing so, the revolutionaries also asserted the specific existence of France as the nation unlike others because it possessed the ideas of the future. France had entered a new order of existence into which only the United States had preceded it, the *novus ordo seclorum* still announced on the Great Seal of the United States.

38   Revolutionary France, and then Napoleonic France, delivered to others the message that it was possible—urgent—for them, too, to rally to this new order of existence, doing so as "nations" that until then did not exist or even know that they should exist, their members still believing themselves part of much larger and less demanding social entities.

The Enlightenment's belief in the possibilities offered by the social and political applications of scientific thought has inspired virtually every political program or doctrine offered since, certainly on the political left, but by no means only there. The doctrinal free-market economic and social policies of the Thatcher and Reagan governments in Britain and the United States in the 1980s firmly claimed to be the application of scientific principles of universal validity.

It was an Enlightenment idea that nature had "linked by an unbreakable chain Truth, Happiness, and Virtue." The challenge was to unlock truth. Communism in the Soviet Union, and in China, Vietnam, Cuba, and elsewhere, engaged in a titanic effort to install as the rule for human affairs what were held to be "invariable natural laws" derived from the scientific interpretation of history. Millions were its victims; but millions too believed in it—including hundreds of thousands, if not millions, of professionally intelligent people, mind-workers, intellectuals, who considered themselves detached and rational persons, above superstition and emotional belief. Yet Communism, among other things, was a secular religion, and its promise of apocalyptic transformation was an essential factor in its success. We know the consequences.

The established form of European political organization in the eighteenth century, dynastic monarchy, whose powers

derived from divine will, was to the Enlightenment mind—
the modern mind—unreasonable, and had to be rejected.
Modern political thought has tried ever since to supply a
generally persuasive and universally valid political theory to
take its place. That of popular self-government, or representative government, is intellectually the most convincing, but
certainly not the most persuasive, if one judges by the numbers of those who have rejected democracy, as against those
who support it. The totalitarian ideological doctrines of the
twentieth century, purportedly based on the "scientific"
knowledge of history, economics, eugenics, and race, were
successfully installed in great nations and produced far
greater cruelty and inhumanity than anything attributable to
monarchy or religious absolutism in the past.

In defiance of experience, an unanalyzed belief in
progress continues to lie at the core of western political
thought today, even though there is no longer a generally
persuasive "scientific" theory of social improvement or
transformation. The belief is unanalyzed because its verifica-
tion and its replacement seem equally impossible tasks. The
implications of what has happened in contemporary history,
and continues to happen, would seem to recommend an intellectual position of historical pessimism, hostile to social
engineering and large programmatic reforms, even when the
program is so modest as simply to enthrone *laissez-faire*—
which has not worked either. But historical pessimism con-
tradicts the principal assumption animating modern western
political society: that it is going someplace, and doing so in
an intelligible way.

The nineteenth century belonged to internationalism:
the internationalism of imperialism. The twentieth century

40   has belonged to nationalism, which has defeated both imperialism and the new internationalisms of Communism and Nazism. Both nationalism and internationalism have been thought by contemporaries to be agencies of progress, as they have been, in the sense that they have advanced us from where we were to where we are. Each has contributed to the conviction that history is going someplace, or should be doing so. But where, and at what costs? This cannot be sensibly discussed in a political vocabulary in which nationalism and internationalism are assigned competitive moral rankings and nations are considered mere steps in the evolutionary rise of society from primeval slime to a radiant future. Too much academic and analytical discussion of nationalism ignores the importance of the communal attachments and conviction of identity (and "authenticity") provided by nationality, and deplores nationalism as an obstacle to progress and liberalism. It may be that. But it is the reality of our century, and needs to be understood in a more complex way than is ordinarily the case. It is a contemporary expression of social and moral realities at the core of human existence.

2 *Nations and Nationalism*

Nationalism is connected with the absence as well as the existence of nations. A violent "nationalism" is often an unsuccessful or unachieved nationalism, the search of a nation to establish political existence, or to separate itself from the foreign political body encompassing it. The nation struggling to be born, in the nature of that situation, is compelled to fight against all that refuses to recognize its claim, occupies what it regards as its national territory, blocks the expression of its national culture or the use of its language. Isaiah Berlin says nationalism "expresses the inflamed desire of the insufficiently regarded to count for something among the cultures of the world." But that puts it meanly, since the nationalism of the great and recognized powers has been as important and damaging a force in modern history as the nationalism of the weak.

Late-nineteenth-century European history was dominated by "the German question," "the Balkan question," and "the eastern question." More recently we have had "the Middle Eastern question," which is the eastern question in a new guise. In 1991, war in what had been Yugoslavia posed once

42 more the Balkan question. All concern the consequences of the breakup of empires or federations and the rise of nations in their place—products of the new force called nationalism. The German question concerned how the German states (more than a thousand of them) which emerged from the breakup of the feudal Holy Roman Empire were to be accommodated in the European system. The German historian Michael Stürmer writes that apart from in the south, where there are the Alps, "Germany has no natural frontiers. The ultimately undefinable legacy of the Holy Roman Empire has left it with frontiers of language, culture, and law which have never coincided with those of [Germany's] dynasties, states, the Empire, or of today's Federal Republic. In other words, Germany was not designed by God and centuries of history but has always had to design itself. In the epoch of the nation-states this is a problem, for Germany is always too small to impose its hegemony, and too big to yield to an equilibrium."

In the mid-nineteenth century Bismarck united most of the German states under Prussia's leadership. He then made war to break the power of rival Austria, and then to defeat France, annexing German-speaking Alsace and Lorraine, proclaiming a second *Reich*, a new German Empire. This was a fundamental challenge by Prussia to the European system of the time, and the eventual result was two world wars.

The German question again found a provisional solution in 1945. Russia on the one hand, and Britain, France, and the United States on the other, cut modern Germany into two states. That new partition was ended in 1990, and still another answer to the German problem was supplied: that of a Germany unified without (most of) Prussia. One would like to believe that this will be the permanent answer.

The Balkan question was never given a satisfactory answer. The issues were frozen between 1945, the end of Hitler's and Stalin's (and Mussolini's) wars in the region, and the collapse of Communism in 1989. Then the question again had to be answered. The earlier, provisional, solution which had been supplied on the initiative of the United States and France in 1918, when the Hapsburg and Ottoman empires came to an end, was universal national self-determination. The application of this principle to the Balkans and to East-Central Europe produced Yugoslavia, "the kingdom of the Serbs, Croats, and Slovenes"; the seventy-four-year existence of modern Czechoslovakia, incorporating Hungarian and German minorities; the restoration of Poland, within controverted borders; the creation of a truncated modern Austria, with a portion of the German-speaking Tyrol nonetheless placed under Italy's rule; and an autonomous Hungary with a majority of ethnic Hungarians left outside. None of this proved a great success. Hitler put a temporary end to it, and Stalin then clamped Soviet control on the entire region (only Austria and Tito's Yugoslavia managed to escape). This situation in turn came to an end in 1989–1991, leaving frontiers intact, as well as the grievances—until the Yugoslav republics, and then the Slovaks, chose to begin their revision.

The development of nationalism in the nineteenth century was connected with the traumas of modernization, which perturbed the social order in parts of the essentially feudal and largely preindustrial Austro-Hungarian and Ottoman empires. Old communities and political attachments were undermined by secularization, urbanization, and the in-

44   fluence of liberal thought, together with the scientists' attack upon religion. This left national attachment as the principal surviving factor in an individual's sense of identity. In the past one had been one or another kind of Christian, or a Moslem, subject of a certain monarch or emperor or territorial magnate. Now each was expected to see himself as member of a nation, even when the nation was indistinct and the accoutrements of nationality had to be manufactured.* The modern Balkan nations and some of those in East-Central Europe were built or rebuilt out of the lumber of history and sometimes of myth. Thus, for example, did modern Greece, Romania, Albania, Czechoslovakia, and reconstituted Serbia come into existence—and even, eventually, Israel. Zionism is the last of East-Central Europe's romantic nationalisms (and a millenarian one: Arthur Hertzberg of New York University and the World Jewish Congress writes of Zionism that its "deepest undercurrent is the conviction that the Zionist state is the transforming event of Jewish history and that it is, at the very least, a preamble to the end of days, in this world").

The new nations were meant to be like the old nations of Western Europe. However, the West European nations had

---

*Not only in the Balkans: The romantic Highland Scot was notoriously the invention of the Lowland-born novelist Sir Walter Scott and of his English admirers who, having forgotten bloody Culloden, were ready to appropriate the Scottish identity as an exotic auxiliary to that of imperial England. The "traditional" kilt and other Scottish regalia prominent at dances, fetes, and weddings in Britain today—and in British industrial conglomerates' advertising of their whisky, and publicizing of their export drives—were largely invented in Queen Victoria's time. Billie Melman of the University of Tel Aviv has also written of the parallel nineteenth-century construction "of an integrative English identity" through the reinventing of an Anglo-Saxon inheritance to offset the actual cosmopolitan Latin-Norman legacy of England, a legacy associated at that time with the threat of revolutionary and Napoleonic France.

not been deliberate inventions but were the accidental product, over a very long time, of the historical development of
peoples who often had little but geographical contiguity in
common. The origin of the French nation, one of the two
original western nation-states, lay in the confused circumstances following the weakening and withdrawal of Roman
power in the regions of continental Europe populated by
Franks, Gallo-Romans, Celts, and Germanic peoples, and the
attempt to re-create a version of "Roman" authority, the only
known form of sophisticated political organization. In the
year 800 the bishop of Rome crowned Charlemagne—the
king of the Franks—as "Holy" Roman Emperor, which is to
say emperor of a reconstituted western and Christian empire.

Charlemagne's successor, Otto (936–973), a German,
was the first claimant to the new imperial title who successfully established a line of succession. The western Roman
Empire thereafter was a German institution, eventually that
of the German Hapsburg dynasty, which renounced the Roman title only in 1806. The fact that modern Germany descends from this empire is the essential reason why Germany
has never become a nation of the kind that France and England are. Germany's historical origin is imperial, not national, the political inheritor of Rome but not of Rome's
language and civilization. Germany in the ninth century was
not the legatee of Greek democracy and Roman republican-
ism, of Roman law and Roman literature. It was a frontier society largely untouched by classical antiquity. This has had
profound consequences in Germany.

The Holy Roman Empire's borders were not fixed, any
more than Rome's had been, or were those of the Church. Its
nature was to expand, and to be inclusive, multinational, and
multilingual. This imperial inclusiveness and proselytizing

46   vocation was responsible for the German knights' crusades
into Baltic and Slavic Europe in order to Christianize pagan
peoples and extend the realm of Christianity. This subsequently became a political undertaking, still understood to
be a civilizing effort. It may be argued that this is why Germany even today experiences a persisting doubt that national
existence can be justified without a missionary purpose or
task, a cause to pursue. The assumed international responsibility or destiny of German civilization was given successive
reformulations in modern times by Goethe, Beethoven,
Frederick the Great, Bismarck, Hegel, William II, Heideg-
ger—and Hitler. In music and philosophy the results were
successful; in politics they were not.

When Bismarck set out to make a powerful imperial
Germany he substituted exclusiveness for the old inclusiveness of the Holy Roman system, and made use of the proposition that there is a German "race." The appropriation of
this Romantic idea that a racial origin identifies nations
proved a decisive factor in Bismarck's enterprise, creating a
new definition and consciousness of German nationality
which have existed ever since. The crisis Germany experienced in 1992–1993 with respect to violence against foreign
demanders of political asylum and its own immigrant worker
population was directly connected to this belief that there is
a German blood identity. The descendants of the "Saxon"
settlers of medieval Romania and Peter the Great's Russia are
thought entitled to automatic citizenship in the Federal Republic even if they have little or no acquaintance with German civilization or do not even speak German. On the other
hand, the children of Turkish or Yugoslav workers in Germany, born and educated in Germany, entirely German in

culture, could be denied citizenship because they were not
German by descent. To obtain German citizenship remains,
for them, an onerous and all but prohibitively lengthy
process.

There certainly are Germanic peoples and Germanic
languages, but as the Yale historian Henry A. Turner has
written, the idea of a German "race" is

a relatively recent invention, having attained widespread acceptance only during the second half of the previous century.
Prior to that, German national identity was defined mainly
in terms of a shared culture, as is still the case in France. And
culture, unlike ethnicity, can be acquired.

Belief in a German ethnic national identity requires denial of historical reality. That country has been a crossroads
and melting pot throughout its past. Over the centuries it has
absorbed large numbers of immigrants—Protestant Hugue-
nots fleeing persecution in France, Dutch settlers willing to
drain swamps, and Poles willing to mine coal. Without the
millions of guest workers enticed to the Federal Republic after World War II from Greece, Italy, Spain and Turkey, the
economic miracle of which Germans are justly proud could
not have taken place.

Early-medieval France, having failed to become the new
Rome, became, instead, one of the two original nation-
states. Instead of the inclusiveness and expansionism of the
empire it acquired the exclusiveness and cultural particularity of the modern nation, and eventually found fixed territorial and linguistic frontiers. There were sovereignties
contemporaneous to early-medieval France which were not
proto-nations, not only Germany but the Constantinian
Empire in the East, and "nations" with a cultural identity but
with no national political definition, or one they were only to

48 achieve later. Feudal society itself was much the same across all the regions that had been part of the Roman Empire or were assimilated into its Christian successor.

The social order rested on agriculture and assumed, and enforced, mutual obligations among peasant farmers or serfs, landholding lords or other local notables, and clergy, within a dominantly religious conception of existence. Society and history provided the arenas in which human salvation had to be worked out. Salvation—the love of God, the achievement of heaven—was the purpose of existence. The church defined the terms of the struggle for salvation, and the social order justified itself by reference to the church. Political authority or sovereignty was a matter of struggle between temporal authorities or lords and the lords of the church. The degree to which a secular political sphere and secular hierarchies emerged depended upon circumstance and place. Independent or quasi-independent cities of merchants, traders, and manufacturers existed within the feudal order, with their own developing claims, and acceptance of obligation.

To reflect on the actual forces that produced the French and English nations is to see how accidental nationhood was, in one respect, and yet how natural it was, even though in neighboring Germany a fundamentally different process was occurring. France and England were defined as nations as a result of the struggle of their feudal princes—rival territorial sovereigns—to consolidate and extend their power through conquest, alliance, or marriage, a general enterprise throughout feudal Europe, nearly as consistently thwarted by the redivisions of power and sovereignties produced by new wars and divided inheritances.

The consolidation of national power first took place on
the two sides of the Channel coast of the continent, in the
cultural context of a linguistic community where French
dominated among the rulers (after 1066) and the people
spoke a number of French, Celtic, and Germanic dialects.
The Norman Conquest of England in the eleventh century
made a French-speaking English dynasty ruler both of England and a part of France (a dynasty Viking in origin, of
course; the "Normans" were Norsemen). This struggle between English and French lords, culminating in the Hundred
Years' War, eventually defined two political nations, divided
by the Channel (but until the sixteenth century not entirely;
England held Calais until 1558) and eventually by language.
English replaced Norman French in the law courts of London only in Tudor times. The outcome of the war left France
under French princes and extended the centralizing powers
of the court. England turned towards the sea, abandoning its
political ambitions on the continent. Both developments
were decisive in the histories of these countries. Two nations
had been created.

Their medieval (and later) conflicts even today influence Franco-British relations, which are never cordial even
when they are cooperative. Today, more than a century and a
half after Napoleon's death, the London popular press re
mains obsessed with the French menace, now allegedly oper-
ating through the mechanisms of the Common Market to
undermine England's independence. The persisting cultural
hostility of the English towards the once-conquering French
is demonstrated in the snobberies of contemporary upper-
class English speech, in which expressions judged "non-U"
(or non-upper-class), as Alan Ross and Nancy Mitford iden-

50   tified them in the mid-1950s, prove consistently to be those
which are French in origin.*

The hostility, interestingly enough, is not reciprocal.
Possibly because the French were the conquerors in 1066,
they are not obsessed with the English. The contemporary
French are inclined to admire the British for their steadfast-
ness, demonstrated in the Second World War, and even for
their style, at least that of the English upper classes, which is
considered chic in France because of its stubborn resistance
to chic.

What happened in England and France provided the
model for political organization elsewhere in Europe. Centralized dynastic states slowly emerged, and from them,
eventually, the modern nation-state, the dominant model of
political, social, and economic organization ever since—
dominant either by the presence of autonomous nationhood
or by its absence, which provokes the forces of unfulfilled nationalism. Contemporary politics remain deeply marked by
efforts to achieve or aggrandize nationhood; yet history in
this century has been more seriously disturbed by efforts to
replace the national organization of society with some new
form of international order—benign or otherwise. It would
be convenient to be able to say that nationalism is a phenomenon of the past, and internationalism that of the future, but
this clearly is not true, and in fact they remain rivals.

In the German lands, the title of Holy Roman Emperor
eventually passed to the Hapsburg monarchy, which, thanks

---

*Stationery for the upper-class *writing paper, chimney* for *fireplace* or *mantel-
piece, mirror* for *looking glass, perfume* for *scent, serviette* for *dinner napkin,
toilet* for what the well-bred call *the loo* (which, alas for consistency, some
say itself comes from the French *lieu,* or "place").

to dynastic marriages, was in time to unite Central Europe with Spain, the Low Countries, and for a time Burgundy. The Hapsburg system also eventually incorporated Bohemia and Poland, nations highly conscious of the independent existence they earlier had possessed, when both were major forces in the development of Central European civilization. Poland was itself a great power in the fifteenth to seventeenth centuries, and was one of the earliest European nation-states. The Hapsburg Empire also included Hungary, and eventually became a "dual" monarchy in which Hungary had nominally equal standing. The ethnically and linguistically distinctive Hungarian nation, of Asian (Finno-Ugric) origin, had established itself in South-Central Europe in the late ninth century. Slovenia and Croatia were also part of the empire, Slovenia as crown land, not an independent nation until 1991. Croatia, an independent state in the early Middle Ages, was from the eleventh century subordinated to Hungary, and like Slovenia became part of the new kingdom of Yugoslavia after the First World War. It briefly reappeared as a state in 1941, under Italian, and later German, Fascist sponsorship, when it distinguished itself by committing monstrous crimes against the neighboring Serbs. The Serbs returned this atrocious favor when the Croatians declared their independence of Yugoslavia in 1991, by invading and attempting to dismember Croatia.

Nation is a deceptively difficult term to define, applicable to peoples as well as to states. Language is frequently held to be the essential element in a nation's existence. Karl Marx defined the nation as possessing a common language, territory, economic life, and common mental makeup (whatever that means: "a common historical formation" might be a better way of putting it). Yet quadrilingual Switzerland is a nation, and so is modern China with all its languages, and probably India is today a nation, and the United States still would be a nation even if it became bilingual and "multicultural"— although it certainly would not be the same nation. On the other hand, Serbs and Croats are the same people and speak the same language, although one writes it in the Cyrillic alphabet and the other in the Roman, and they certainly are today not one nation but two. What has divided them is religion and the related phenomenon that history put one in the conquered Byzantine/Ottoman world and the other into the cultural universe of Western Europe.

The great nineteenth-century historian Lord Acton speaks of "national" sentiment as first exhibited in resistance to the French Revolution's universalizing ideas and the revolutionary and Napoleonic armies' efforts to impose French rule abroad. However, after the defeat of Napoleon, "[n]ationality, which the old regime had ignored, which had been outraged by the revolution and the empire, received, after its first open demonstration, the hardest blow at the Congress of Vienna. . . . The governments of the Holy Alliance devoted themselves to suppress with equal care the revolutionary spirit by which they had been threatened, and the national spirit by which they had been restored." The liberal movement which subsequently developed in resistance to the reactionary alliance of Europe's restored monarchies "began in defense of liberty, religion, and nationality. All these causes were united in the Irish agitation, and in the Greek, Belgian, and Polish revolutions." The Turks, Dutch, and Russians "were attacked, not as usurpers, but as oppressors—because they misgoverned, not because they were of a different race. Then began a time when the text simply was, that nations would not be governed by foreigners. . . . National rights, like religion, had borne part in the previous combinations, and had been auxiliaries in the struggles for freedom, but now nationality became a paramount claim which . . . was to prevail at the expense of every other cause for which nations make sacrifices." It was, Acton concludes, "a retrograde step in history."

Acton also writes, "The combination of different nations in one state is as necessary a condition of civilized life as the combination of men in society. . . . A state which is incompetent to satisfy different races condemns itself; a state which labors to neutralize, to absorb, or to expel them, destroys its own vitality; a state which does not include them is destitute of the chief basis of self-government." The idea that nations have a racial origin (or, to employ the current expression, a singular "ethnic" origin) is generally untenable. Daniel Bell, writing in the context of a larger conception of ethnicity, has argued that the state "is an effective unit of identification [and therefore of competition] where there is a congruence between the nation and a single primordial group." But what is a primordial group? There was no ethnic primordial group for the English or French nations, the oldest of the modern nations, nor for any other major West European nation. Ethnically homogeneous Scandinavia, which lay off the track of the successive Central Asian migrations that swept through Central Europe and produced its ethnic mix, nonetheless possesses three ancient nations, which fought with one another for centuries.

Carlton J. H. Hayes, the distinguished American scholar, said that nationality is the product of remembered or imagined factors from a people's past which together produce the conviction of being a separate and distinct part of

54   mankind. (The joke has been made that a nation is a people
united by a common dislike of its neighbors and a common
mistake about its origins.) Nationalism is an emphasis upon
this distinctness at the expense of the similarities of mankind
as a whole, and for that reason easily becomes an aggressive
attempt to impose the difference as a superiority. Hayes was
particularly concerned by the tendency of nationalism to
adopt patriotic rituals which resemble those of religion, ele-
vating the state as giver of private as well as public morality,
and thus making the state into a simulacrum of the Deity. In
Hayes's time (he died in 1964, at eighty-two) this tendency
had produced the worship of state in Germany and the can-
onization of ideology in Russia: with both ersatz gods requiring blood sacrifice. However, this worship of state or party in
the two great totalitarian movements of the century involves
more complex issues than nationalism itself—or so I will argue in the following chapter.

The British academics Eric Hobsbawm and Isaiah
Berlin, men of a generation formed by the liberal tradition,
find nationalism's exaltation of one people over others so unreasonable, and the values of internationalism so com-
pellingly reasonable, that they have difficulty accepting that
intelligent people could be nationalists. Nationalism's apparent illogicality suggests to them that it must eventually and
naturally disappear, as an aberrant phenomenon, destroyed
by progress. Berlin also sees in it an affront to a utopianism
based on Enlightenment values which expresses man's most
admirable hopes, a utopianism Berlin wanted to believe in
but was compelled to reject as unrealizable and philosophi-
cally illusory.

He speaks of Tolstoy's belief "that the essence of human

beings was to be able to choose how to live: societies could be
transformed in the light of true ideas believed in with enough
fervor and dedication." In this perspective he finds nationalism a monstrous and primitive force of false ideals, even
though these may be held with the same "fervor and dedication" as the ideals of the utopian. But Freud, the bleak realist,
said, "It is always possible to bind together a considerable
number of people in love, so long as there are other people
left over to receive the manifestations of their aggressiveness."

Berlin would certainly have been distressed by the fact
that tenured university professors, including the dean of the
school of science at Sarajevo University (a woman), an eminent professor of literature, and a psychiatrist, were leaders
of the Serbian "autonomous" republic proclaimed inside
Bosnia-Herzegovina in 1992, and supervised the heartless
siege of Sarajevo and the genocidal ethnic purges of those
parts of Bosnia their followers conquered. One would think
it evident by now that intelligent, or at least educated, people
have as well documented a disposition as any others to pursue ideological programs in defiance of pragmatic judgment,
evidence, or common morality. On the utopians' side, the
evidence for this is provided by the seven-decade-long infat-
uation with Leninism of an important part of the West's intelligentsia.

Contemporary academic discussions of nationalism
have treated it as a force in the development and modernization of a political society, or they have tried—without success, in my view—to fit it into a progressive or Marxist
conception of historical evolution, in order to demonstrate
that it is transitional or non-essential. Liah Greenfeld of
Harvard argues that nationality is fundamentally conceptual

56   or ideological, as well as independent of ethnicity, and that
the United States is the model of modernization, which
would seem to underestimate the degree to which American
national identity is presently in doubt, placing in question its
validity as a model of modern nationhood.

Ernest Gellner, a Cambridge (England) social anthropologist, says nationalism is the product of modern society's
need for "universal, standardized, generic education," the result of "a *certain kind* of division of labor" characteristic of
the modern world, "complex, but also perpetually, and often
rapidly, changing." As this form of education is possible only
when state and culture are linked, society produces such a
linkage. "That is what nationalism is about." Premodern societies which fail to develop the necessary identification of
state with culture fail, and are taken over by more successful
societies. As nationalist conflict is the result of "social
chasms created by early industrialism, and by the unevenness
of its diffusion," Gellner concludes that late industrial society "can be expected to be one in which nationalism persists,
but in a muted, less virulent form." This was written before
the fall of Communism and the events of 1991 and after.

Benedict Anderson of Cornell University says the development of the printing press and the standardization of languages, and the emergence of written vernacular literatures
which followed, made possible "imagined communities"
much grander than the actual ones which existed before, and
for this reason the modern nation developed, and with it national consciousness, and eventually nationalism. The bourgeois intelligentsia brought into being by the print
revolution "invited the masses into history" (a nice phrase,
which Anderson takes from another Marxist, Tom Nairn).
He claims that the rise of nationalism has coincided with the

decline of religion as a social force, but this seems misleading
in its implication, since the decline of popular religious belief in Europe occurred during the late nineteenth and the
twentieth centuries, while nationalism first gained force in
the early nineteenth century, and remains particularly powerful in the regions of Eastern and Southern Europe the least
touched by disbelief and secular ideas.

In Asia and Africa (which I will discuss in a later chapter), nationalism—Gandhi's India is the possible exception—
nearly always has been an affair of the secularized elites. The
languages of African "nationalism" are English and French.
On the other hand, contemporary Islamic religious fundamentalism is best understood as a response to the failure of
secular nationalist movements in the Middle East in the
1950s and after. Tom Nairn, a Scot, is perhaps representative
of all the academic analysts in holding that nationalism is "a
pathology." He nonetheless considers it inevitable in modern
historical development, just as neurosis is an element in personal development.

None of this seems to me convincing as an explanation
of nationalism, which does not need complicated explanations. Its links to the primordial human attachments to family, clan, and community seem obvious. A Canadian of
Russian origin, the novelist and journalist Michael Ignatieff,
wrote in the autumn of 1992 of a Sunday in St. George's
Cathedral in Lvov, in Ukraine: ". . . the church is packed
with bareheaded men and kerchiefed women of all ages, and
when they join the choir in the Alleluia, the sound floats
above seven hundred heads, like a gently billowing canopy.
Standing among men and women who do not hide intense,
long-suppressed feelings, it becomes clear what nationalism

58 really is: the dream that a whole nation could be like a con-
gregation—singing the same hymns, listening to the same
gospel, sharing the same emotions, linked not only to each
other but to the dead buried beneath their feet."

The nineteenth-century French scholar Ernest Renan
argued that it is "will" which makes a nation. A nation is "a
daily plebiscite," "a spiritual principle," "a moral consciousness." It is a community with a common memory—a people
which has suffered together. In a famous phrase in his 1882
lecture "What Is a Nation?" he said that the "essence of a nation is that its people have much in common and have forgotten much." He continued: "Every French citizen ought to
have forgotten Saint Bartholomew's Day [the mass murder of
Protestants on that day in 1572] and the thirteenth-century
massacres of the Midi [of Albigensian heretics, by the Inqui-
sition]." That is to say, for the French nation to thrive, its citizens must deliberately put behind them events which have
divided them.

The most practical definition of a nation probably is
that of the most eminent of contemporary students of nationalism, the late Hugh Seton-Watson, and it resembles that
of Renan. Seton-Watson wrote that after a lifetime of study
he was "driven to the conclusion that no 'scientific definition' of a nation can be devised; yet the phenomenon has existed and exists. All that I can find to say is that a nation exists
when a significant number of people in a community consider themselves to form a nation, or behave as if they formed
one. It is not necessary that the whole of the population
should so feel, or so behave, and it is not possible to lay down
dogmatically a minimum proportion of a population which
must be so affected. When a significant group holds this belief, it possesses 'national consciousness.'"

3 *Internationalism*

The past was more "internationalist" than we have any conclusive evidence the future will be. Tribal society or the primitive agricultural hamlet of preantiquity was not replaced by nation but by city, or by a city-based civilization which enlarged itself so as to become an empire with non-exclusionary frontiers. This was followed by the development of universal religions—Judaism, Christianity, and later Islam—in the Mediterranean world.

Dynastic monarchy or empire—polyglot, multicommunal, multinational—was the characteristic political institution of Europe before the Enlightenment and the French Revolution. It formed and redivided territorially and communally according to monarchical succession, marriages, and wars. The Austrian novelist Joseph Roth wrote in *Hotel Savoy* (1924) of

the Count Franz Xaver Morstin, the scion of an old Polish family, a family which . . . originated in Italy and came to Poland in the sixteenth century. . . . [H]e thought of himself neither as a Polish aristocrat nor as an aristocrat of Italian origin . . . [but as] one of the noblest and purest sort of Austrian, plain and simple. That is, a man above nationality, and

60 therefore of true nobility. Had anyone asked him, for example—but to whom would such a senseless question have occurred?—to which "nationality" or race he felt he belonged,
the Count would have felt rather bewildered, baffled even, by
his questioner, and probably bored and somewhat indignant.
And on what indications might he have based his membership of this or that race? He spoke almost all European languages equally well, he was at home in almost all the
countries of Europe. His friends and relations were scattered
about the wide colorful world. . . . One of his brothers-in-
law was District Commandant in Sarajevo, another was
Counsellor to the Governor in Prague; one of his brothers
was serving as an *Oberleutnant* of artillery in Bosnia, one of
his cousins was Counsellor of Embassy in Paris, another was
a landowner in the Hungarian Banat, a third was in the Italian diplomatic service and a fourth, from sheer love of the
Far East, had for years lived in Peking.

We are talking about an Austro-Hungarian, of course,
subject of the successor to the Roman Empire, by way of the
Hapsburg possession of the Holy Roman Emperor's title.
However, the continental aristocracy elsewhere was also international in views and family alliances, as were the monarchies. The British monarchy today is German in family
origin, and because of Prince Philip will be half Greek if
Philip's son Charles becomes king; except, of course, that the
Greek royal house actually is Danish and Russian, while that
of Denmark is Hessian, and English before that, as well as
German and Swedish. . . .

The Hapsburgs, originally Alsatian-Swiss, from the
thirteenth to the twentieth century ruled not only German
Austria, and at times Hungary, Bohemia, Poland, Lombardy,
and Tuscany, and a part of the Balkans, but Spain, Belgium,
and the Netherlands (hence the magnificent Flemish and

Dutch paintings in Vienna and Madrid today). Normans, **61**
originally Vikings, conquered England but also ruled Sicily
and Sardinia. The French Bourbons ruled France from 1589
to 1792 (or to 1830, counting the Restoration), and the family's branches ruled Sicily, Naples, Parma, and Spain, where
they intermarried with the Hapsburgs. King Juan Carlos of
Spain is a Bourbon, as is the consort of the claimant to the
throne of Romania, Michael.

The peasant of premodern Europe thought of himself as
a Christian—as opposed to a Moor or Turk or Jew—but politically he was simply a subject of this or that prince or local
magnate, or of a distant emperor; he surely was not conscious
of himself as member of a nation in the modern sense. The
internationalism of the twentieth century, with its UN, its
League of Nations, even its European Community, provides
an impoverished comparison to the pervasive internationalism of medieval society.

The Eastern Roman Empire, in Constantinople, equally
international, dominated the Balkan peninsula (modern
Greece, Serbia, Macedonia, Bulgaria, and Romania) as well
as modern Turkey, and ruled most of the southern Mediterranean coast, including North Africa, Egypt, Palestine,
Syria, and also a part of Italy, and for a time Rome itself. After the rise of the Arab Empire and the break (in 1054) between Roman and Orthodox Christianities, this Byzantine
empire lost its claim to universality but remained a considerably more subtle and complex civilization than Western Europe at the time. It delivered Christianity to Russia by way of
Bulgaria. The Byzantine state collapsed when Constantinople fell to the Ottoman Turks in 1453.

It had lacked the political virtues of the Roman Republic

62   and Greek democracies which were its antecedents. The office of Roman emperor had originated in a free people's delegation of powers over the *res publica*, or public "things" or affairs, but this by the third and fourth centuries became in Western Europe an institution in which power was considered the personal possession of the emperor. The empire in the East became transformed into what the English historian Ernest Barker describes as "an absolute and quasi-Asiatic monarchy, under which all its subjects fell into a single level of legal submission." The emperor's was "a gorgeous court, marked by all the ceremony and the servility of the East." When Constantinople fell to the Ottoman Turks in 1435 the eastern Christian church survived by northward migration, with Moscow eventually becoming the new metropolis of Orthodoxy, and the Russian czar ("Caesar") becoming, effectively, the successor to the eastern emperor. (Hence the idea of Moscow as "the third Rome," which has weighed so heavily on the Russians' subsequent approach to the world.)

The character of the Byzantine employment of power across the many "nations" of the empire made the fortunes, interests, and sometimes the survival of the emperor's subjects dependent upon family, clan, and communal attachments and alliances. Dissimulation, indirection, and pliancy if not obsequiousness in dealing with power were qualities of survival, and certainly of success. The influence of this politico-cultural inheritance is discernible in all the once-Byzantine countries. (As these included Sardinia, Sicily, Corsica, and a part of mainland Italy, there is a sense in which the Mafia can be called a product of Byzantium.)*

*On the other hand, the Sicilian-American Mafia leader Joe Bonanno, in his memoirs, published in 1983, describes the Mafia of the 1930s as a way of life "which precedes the formation of city-states and later of nations."

The "universal empire" of the Arabs, which erupted out of the desert with a new, prophetic, and proselytizing religion, was first centered in Damascus, then in Baghdad, at one point ruling nearly from China on the one side to Spain and southern France on the other. Like Byzantium, it was multinational, as was the succeeding Ottoman Empire, which incorporated Christians of several varieties and Jews (in an inferior status, to be sure), Greeks, Bulgars, Serbs, Macedonians, and eventually Hungarians; as well as Moslems: Arabs, Egyptians, Bosnians, Albanians, and so on.

The First World War put an end to Europe's internal empires, the Ottoman, Austro-Hungarian, and Prussian. The czarist empire became Bolshevik, and survived until 1989. The Second World War ended the European overseas empires. The world has not recovered from the consequences of either event. The First World War could be called nationalism's victory over the prevailing internationalism of prewar society, in which passports were largely unknown and Europe's elites were international in their assumptions and attachments. Yet at the same time nationalism was generally identified as a cause of the war: the national "power politics" and national self-aggrandizement of the European states. The reaction among the Allied powers was to put forward a postwar form of liberal internationalism, identified with the United States' Woodrow Wilson and the French statesman Aristide Briand. This produced the League of Nations and its associated agencies, and the Kellogg-Briand agreement of 1928, by which the contracting parties (eventually sixty-two nations ratified the agreement) renounced war as an instrument of national policy.

However, this liberal internationalism also failed. It was

64   undermined by national rivalries among the newly created or
newly confirmed states occupying the place of the old Hapsburg and Ottoman systems, but was finally destroyed by Fascist nationalism and Nazi internationalism, the most
powerful political forces at work in Europe between 1918 and
1942. Nazism was an internationalist ideology, based on
racial categorization and racial myth. Italian Fascism was a
doctrine of will and mastery which made a great appeal to
radical nationalist circles elsewhere in interwar Europe, but
was essentially an expression of Italian national affirmation
and expansionism, ambitious to re-create an Italian empire
on the model of Rome.

The other important internationalism of the period was
Bolshevism, or Communist internationalism, based on class
theory and a pseudoscientific millenarianism. It had a great
influence on what (misleadingly) is described as Asian nationalism, as well as among the secularized western intelligentsia of the period, a significant number of whom became
its uncritical converts. Raymond Aron once wrote that
(mere) "reform, once accomplished, changes something. A
revolution seems capable of changing everything, since no
one knows precisely what it will change." Communist internationalism was the product of the revolutionary thought of
Karl Marx, a man of Enlightenment Europe, his intellectual
tradition, in Sidney Hook's words, "Greek and scientific . . . his ethical ideal a society 'in which the free development of each is the condition of the free development of all.'
Ultimately the test of all institutions was the extent to which
they made possible for all persons the full and rich development of their personalities." Marx was convinced of the ultimate triumph of science and reason in history. The purpose

of his life and work was to establish a science of society as reliable as the natural science already triumphantly interpret-
ing the nineteenth century material order.

However, implicit in his work was a fateful secular translation of the messianism of his Jewish religious origins. His
confidence in his interpretation of the ultimately benign
evolutionary operations of history was such that he argued,
"A social state never dies before there has been fully developed within it the sum of all the productive forces that it con-
tains. New relations in production, superior to the former
ones, never come into being before their material reason for
existence has developed in the womb of the old society."
However, as Edmund Stillman and I have argued elsewhere,
despite Marx's claim that these were scientific conclusions,

the inner impulse that drove him to construct his revolutionary theories was more obscure, drawing, it may be, upon the
sources of Biblical prophecy and medieval eschatology. In
any case, it was the Marx of Old Testament prophecy—the
poet of God's wrath on the world—and not the Marx of sci-
entism and unnatural faith who proved the more reliable
prophet. The optimistic visions of Marx remain unfulfilled.
But his darker visions of social decay and social convulsion
have figured as a prophecy to whose fulfillment it itself con-
tributes, a prophecy of the dissolution of the nineteenth-
century world, and a stimulus to disorder in the twentieth
century.*

Marxism said that the dialectical process governing history, by which higher forms of social organization replaced
lesser ones, had its foreordained eventual outcome in a millennial reign of justice, embodied in the rule of the prole-

---

*The Politics of Hysteria (1964).

66   tariat. This promise proved capable of enlisting generations of the idealistic, exploiting and squandering their idealism in what one might have thought the implausible proposition that a decisive break with the human past could be produced, an abolition of the human condition—even of human mortality, since the triumphant proletariat would prove immortal. From the later nineteenth century to the 1990s appalling suffering and death were inflicted on millions as a consequence of this doctrine, and of its application to society by Lenin, Stalin, Mao Tse-tung and their collaborators and successors. Tens of thousands of people selflessly gave themselves to its propagation, missionaries of the proposition the poet W. H. Auden stated (in words he later retracted) as "[t]he conscious acceptance of guilt in the necessary murder." In Auden's defense, one must add that the vocation of the poet is to be a witness to his time, not its political analyst. In this respect it is interesting that both Marx and Engels had "set out in their youth to be poets." Both, unfortunately, were to choose politics as their medium of expression—as Hitler, the painter and architect *manqué*, was later to do. (In Hitler's case, he had first to level his building site.)

Communism purported to offer an objective science of society and a scientific program for class action and collective progress. Its great twentieth-century rival, Nazism, was based on the opposite conviction, that of the primacy of man's "organic" and instinctual attachments, impelling him towards fulfillment in communal or national or racial solidarity, and in heroic actions. The Nazi program envisaged Europe's unification under the Nordic peoples: the Germans, the Scandinavians, the Dutch—and the English. This is why Germany's occupation of the Netherlands, Denmark, and Norway was "correct," mostly respecting recognized norms of military occupation, while in the East it was genocidal. It is why Hitler so bitterly resented the refusal of the British, under Churchill, to agree to a global settlement after Dunkirk that would have given Britain rule of the seas and its empire—its own sovereignty over "inferior" peoples—leaving Europe to Germany.

While Nazism exploited national sentiment and the resentments of the "national movement" in Weimar Germany, making dramatic use of a theater and rhetoric of nationalism, it was fundamentally an internationalist ideology based on racialist theory. It conceived of itself as the vehicle of Aryan "Nordic" (not specifically German) supremacy over inferior races, of which the Jews were merely one—if, in Nazi eyes, the most powerful and dangerous. The Slavs were also inferior, thought fit only to labor under Nordic domination. Shortly after his invasion of Russia, Hitler told the Japanese ambassador to Berlin of his "General Plan for the East." He said (the historian Klaus Hildebrand writes) that his intention was "to settle Poland, the Baltic States, White Russia and part of the Ukraine with Germans over a period of thirty years: 31 million of the existing population were to be deported to western Siberia, and 14 million of 'good stock' permitted to remain."*

Gypsies, homosexuals and sexual deviants were "degenerate" and deserved extinction, like the Jews. This was a mat-

---

*The black and brown races scarcely entered into Hitler's plans, which centered on Europe, but Africans would certainly have been enslaved or the effort made to exterminate them had they come under Hitler's power. One reason Hitler before 1943–1944 largely disregarded the United States as a factor in the war was that even a racially segregated America—as it was then—was considered by him a "mongrel" nation, its military potential therefore negligible.

68   ter of social or racial eugenics. The mentally deficient and physically crippled had also to be put down in order to purify the human stock. Hitler's euthanasia program to eliminate "worthless life" began in peacetime with incurable German invalids its subjects. The first experiments with gas chambers were made in connection with that program, which was halted in 1942 because word of it had got out and there were protests from both Catholic and Protestant church officials. Hitler's angry response was that "the German people was not yet mature enough for the policy he had designed for it." Again to quote Hildebrand, Hitler's ambition, "misunderstood as conservative, [was] in fact revolutionary . . . to create a new type of humanity by means of global and racial conquest and eugenic methods, within the framework of a 'Greater German Reich.' " His actual view of the Germans was expressed in his statement in the summer of 1944, as defeat was approaching, that he doubted that the German people were "worthy of my ideals." Germans were means to his ends. He was no German nationalist.

Considering the origins of Nazism, Hannah Arendt has observed that it is an "outrageous fact" that "so small (and, in world politics, so unimportant) a phenomenon as the Jewish question and anti-semitism could become the catalytic agent for first, the Nazi movement, then a world war, and finally the establishment of death factories." However, it was no more outrageous than that an avowedly humane undertaking to rescue the industrial working class from powerlessness and exploitation should have resulted in the Gulag, with more victims than the Nazi camps, vast purges of the innocent, and the political institutionalization for the better part of a century of lies and betrayal.

Anti-Semitism has been a non-rational force in the western consciousness and in western politics since the Middle Ages, disconnected from what Jews individually or collectively have actually done or do. Despite Hitler's defeat and the example of the death camps, it remains such a force today. Indeed, it may be more extensive today than before the Second World War, when it was a phenomenon largely limited to Europe and the European-populated Americas. Anti-Zionism and hostility to Israel, and by extension hostility to Jews as such, now is powerful throughout the Islamic world, and to a lesser but important extent in the non-western societies generally, where anti-imperialism, anti-westernism, anti-Zionism, and anti-Semitism have now become all but hopelessly intertwined with one another. Even Japan, which does not have, and has never had, any experience of Jews, now manifests a form of anti-Semitism, connected to allegations of global Zionist conspiratorial power as bizarre as those made in the notorious nineteenth-century forgery *The Protocols of the Elders of Zion.*

According to Hannah Arendt, who is, I think, entirely convincing on this matter, the second major influence on the development of Nazism as a doctrine was nineteenth-century imperialism, by means of which the limits of the nation were slipped and power sought internationally—transnationally. "Expansion is everything," Cecil Rhodes said, despairing at the stars: "these vast worlds which we can never reach. I would annex the planets if I could." Realists in nineteenth-century government opposed imperialism. They were not inconsiderable figures. Bismarck, Clemenceau, and Gladstone all opposed the imperialist parties in their countries because, as Arendt said, they grasped that imperial expansion "could only destroy the political body of the nation-state," since the

THE WRATH OF NATIONS

70 nation-state, "based upon a homogeneous population's active consent to its government," could not integrate a colonial population as the earlier forms of inclusive and non-national empires could.* As the modern empires did not invite their African or Indonesian or Indian subjects to say, "*Civis Romanus sum*," but instead merely to submit to foreign domination, their essential tendency was towards inequity and tyranny, however powerful the paternalistic and missionary impulses of the colonizers may also have been.

In retrospect, Nazism is commonly thought to have entirely lacked the ostensible altruism and humanitarian ambitions that enabled international Communism to make such a powerful appeal to the elites of the 1920s to 1950s. This is not true. Nazism had its idealism of Nietzschean mastery, and its social idealists, however appallingly it all ended. S. J. Woolf says that the "socialist or corporativist claims of fascism" made by the Italian "revolutionary syndicalists and corporatists, [in] the very name of the German National Socialist Party, [and by] the Spanish vertical syndicates [and] the Portuguese national syndicalists, [and] Mosley's driving concern with the problem of unemployment left contemporaries bewildered and have sometimes made historians uncertain

---

*This observation obviously is important with respect to the tension experienced in many European countries today as a result of immigration from their former colonies, and it also emphasizes the overall success of the United States in creating a kind of internal, inclusive "empire" in which immigrants have until recently nearly all been successfully integrated. Whether this will continue to be the case in the future is a question of great importance for the United States. There is dispiriting evidence that it may not, and of course there are many now in the United States who say that it should not, that the cultural assimilation of immigrants is a form of cultural aggression. This, in my opinion, is a sentimental and unhistorical opinion, and a threat to the country's future.

about where to locate fascism in the political spectrum."

In his wartime novel *Arrival and Departure*, Arthur Koestler (himself Jewish and a Zionist) has one of his characters, a young Nazi diplomat, describe Nazism as "a real revolution and more internationalist in its effects than the storming of the Bastille or of the Winter Palace in Petrograd. . . . Every new, cosmopolitan idea in History has first to be adopted by one particular nation, become a national monopoly as it were, and become formulated in nationalist terms before it can begin its universal expansion. . . ." The young Nazi speaks of the future integration of Europe's resources, industries, energy, and transportation, the stripping away of restrictions and abolishing of frontiers, in a way that anticipates what actually has happened since 1945 in the course of Europe's economic unification and creation of a Single European Market. "[W]e are experimenting," he concludes, "but experimenting on a scale never dreamt of before. We have embarked on something—something grandiose and gigantic beyond imagination. There are no more impossibilities for man now."

Such a program could easily appeal to French, Danish, or Belgian patriots who hated the parliamentary corruptions of prewar politics, the "mediocrity" of societies devoted to money and material satisfactions. They could convince themselves that their nations would find purification in their reconstitution as part of Hitler's gigantic pan-European experiment. J. Delperrié de Bayac, a historian of Vichy France's collaborationist political police, the Milice, writes of the Vichy cabinet official in charge of this unit, Joseph Darnand: "Darnand had never known any Germans. He had never met them on the battlefield. He did not like them, and fundamentally, he never liked them. But he felt the highest degree

72   of attraction to a victorious Nazism. With a perfectly good conscience (had not Marshal Pétain shown the way?) he persuaded himself that France, in order to save itself and find a rebirth, had to become Nazi."

The argument that the interwar movements of the radical Right were forms of extreme nationalism is better made of Italian Fascism than of Nazism, although Fascism too proved an international phenomenon. Mussolini was not only an early influence on Hitler but on Fascist or fascistic movements emerging in Hungary, Romania, Spain, Latin America, and elsewhere. However, this influence was essentially stylistic and tactical, an emphasis on action and on the subordination of individuals to an exalted notion of the national interest or a nation's destiny. The political objectives of all the Fascist movements remained fundamentally nationalistic, not internationalist and racist as in the case of Hitler. The British Fascist leader Oswald Mosley wrote in his autobiography (1968): "Never talk to me about a fascist International, for the peace of Europe might have been maintained if such an organization had existed. If our continent had found a reasonable measure of union through a new European spirit, instead of division by the old nationalism, twenty-five million people might be alive today and Europe the greatest power in the world." Mosley never admitted that the character and aims of that internationalism, as Hitler conceived it, required those twenty-five million deaths. The united Europe actually created after 1945 was made by Jean Monnet, Robert Schuman, Konrad Adenauer, Alcide De Gasperi, and others—all liberal politicians, most of them Catholics: men of qualities any proper Fascist would have despised as weaknesses.

●

The basis of the nineteenth- and twentieth-century Left's internationalism was the assumption, following Marx, that the interests of workers (and of owners, and *rentiers*, as social classes) are international in character. The First International, created in London in 1864 by British, French, German, Italian, Swiss, and Polish delegates, collapsed in 1871 because of the popular revulsion in Europe against the reported atrocities of the Paris Commune, whose leadership had included a number of the First International's prominent figures.

The Second International, founded in Paris in 1889, on the centenary of the French Revolution, was destroyed by the twentieth century's greatest war of nationalism, in 1914, when the German Social Democratic party proved incapable of resisting the frantic patriotism of the moment. Socialist party deputies "would have been trampled to death in front of the Brandenburg Gate" had they failed to approve war credits, a contemporary observed; however, the truth was that the Socialists shared the general enthusiasm for war. In peace they had sung "The Internationale" and proclaimed belief in the solidarity of the international working class, but at the end of July and the beginning of August 1914 they proved no different from Germans of all elements of society, discovering in the flood of patriotic emotion that accompanied mobilization what the great historian Friedrich Meinecke could describe thirty-five years later, despite all the disasters that had followed, as perhaps the most "sublime" days of his life.

German and French Socialists, with the majority of the British Labour movement, went to war in 1914 with enthusiasm. The British Fabian movement divided, with Ramsay MacDonald leading a pacifist and internationalist wing while

74   Arthur Henderson, leader of the Labour party, entered the coalition war government. Socialist theory and internationalist idealism were overtaken and destroyed by primordial emotions of communal solidarity and identification—other names for nationalism—and no doubt by the force of Thanatos as well, that dark willingness, even eagerness, to die as well as to kill, which erupts in human communities and is a force permanently at work in history.

The Third International, created in 1919 by the Soviet Communist party, was merely an instrument of Soviet foreign policy, although it enlisted powerful internationalist sentiments and exploited a wealth of altruism and idealism. It ended in the Second World War, when Stalin nakedly subordinated international Communist interests to Soviet national interests. Lenin had been an internationalist who considered Russia a backward country. He thought his revolution could not survive unless supporting revolutions followed in more advanced industrial countries with large industrial proletariats. He expected this first of all in Germany. R. N. Carew-Hunt writes that "[h]is advocacy of revolution was not even remotely connected in his mind with the territorial aggrandizement of Russia." But Stalin, who knew little of the world outside Russia (where he had been only twice before coming to power: to Bolshevik party congresses in Stockholm and London in 1906 and 1907), took for granted the subordination of international Communism's interests to those of Russia. Eventually, under him, "cosmopolitanism" became a capital crime.

The willingness of a significant part of an avowedly atheistic twentieth-century intelligentsia to commit itself to Communism, an ostensibly scientific yet transparently naive

simulacrum of messianic religion, merits sober attention as
an example of a recurrent factor in political existence.* The
young men and women of the worldwide Communist movement—underground activists in Britain and the United
States, spying against their own governments; Comintern
militants preparing the revolution in Germany and France;
poets joining industrial workers and peasants to fight Franco
in Spain; intellectuals organizing the powerless in China and
Vietnam; artists writing "proletarian" novels and painting
"progressive" paintings—these were the Jesuits of the twentieth century. But unlike Jesuits, they were prepared to at-
tribute omniscience and infallibility to their fellow-men,
Lenin, Stalin, and Mao Tse-tung, rather than to a God outside history and time.

How are we to explain this, or comprehend its implications, which are very grave, as we have no particular reason
to think that the phenomenon will not recur? Is it the result
of a simple need to believe? Or of the impulse to sacrifice
oneself? The need for a doctrine to make life intelligible?
The First World War offers a part of the explanation, of
course. That catastrophe had seemed to demonstrate the
bankruptcy of the political system which had prevailed in
Europe before 1914 and had produced such a war. The Great
Depression after 1929 seemed evidence of an equivalent failure of capitalism. Nonetheless, how remote, even incredible,
it is that hundreds of thousands of serious people could have
believed, for example—as Leon Trotsky wrote in 1931—that
the struggle in China between those former allies, the Communist party and Chiang Kai-shek's Kuomintang, was "in-

*A character in Umberto Eco's novel *Foucault's Pendulum* describes Marxism as "an apocalyptic cult that came out of the Trier region. Am I right?"

76   comparably more important for human culture and destiny than the vain and pitiful babel of Europe's parliaments and the mountains of literature produced by stagnant civilizations." Revolution, Trotsky went on, "is a stage in the development of society conditioned by objective causes and subject to determined laws, so that a scientific intelligence is able to foresee the general direction of the process. Only the study of the anatomy of a society and of its physiology makes possible a reaction to events that is based on scientific forecasts rather than the conjectures of dilettantes."

Until the late 1980s, when the evidence of Communism's collapse became irrefutable, many who were the enemies of Communism believed nearly as ardently as the Communists themselves in the power of Marxist doctrine. Until very recently there were many in the West who were convinced that only war could end Communism—that "universal evil," as Aleksandr Solzhenitsyn said in 1982. Great risks had to be run if its power was to be checked. The marvelous Italian novelist Ignazio Silone—a Communist, and later a Christian, revolutionary—said in the 1940s that history's "final battle" would be between the Communists and the ex-Communists. Only they were equipped to understand the struggle. The rest of us were "dilettantes."

Marxism was the work of an intellectually ambitious journalist (sometime editor of the *Rheinische Zeitung* and free-lancer for *The New York Tribune*, ancestor of today's *International Herald Tribune)* greatly influenced by Hegel's belief that a "world soul" exists and develops by a dialectical process. It was developed as a revolutionary program by other journalists—Lenin, Trotsky (journalism then was the way revolutionaries made a living; today it is by teaching in universities). The result in 1918 and after was a catastrophic transformation of the course of twentieth-century history. The immense social and material damage it produced is still with us; the millions of tortured and dead are gone. Its success invites the bleakest judgment on man and politics, tempered only by the fact that, in the end, defeating it did not require war; it collapsed. The force that caused it to collapse was nationalism.

Nationalism destroyed both these novel and totalitarian forms of despotic internationalism, Nazism and Communism. They were resisted because they were evil, certainly: their cruelty, and dehumanizing force, awaked moral resistance everywhere they touched. But the fundamental political force mobilizing resistance to Hitler was nationalism, and this was true long before even Germany's enemies had grasped the real nature of Nazism and its genocidal aims. Churchill's indomitable Englishness, his ability to mobilize the British people by means of a soaring rhetoric of patriotism and evocation of history; the appeal of de Gaulle to "a certain idea" of France "as dedicated to an exalted and exceptional destiny"; the patriotism of Dutch, Belgians, Norwegians, Czechs, Poles, and the others prepared to fight on in 1940 and 1941, when victory was impossible to foresee, and Russia was a German ally and the United States remote and isolationist—all this was what halted Hitler and prepared his eventual defeat.

Moreover, when the U.S.S.R. and the United States did enter the war, their motives were national survival and national revenge, after being attacked. The victory of the Soviet Union in 1945 was widely taken at the time to be a validation of the "scientific" socialism professed by the

78 U.S.S.R., but it should have been evident even then that nationalism, people's attachment to place and a particular history, had actually been the essential motivation for the Soviet peoples' resistance to Germany. Stalin himself provided the evidence for this by naming the war "the Great Patriotic War." Nationalism proved as well to be the source of resistance to the postwar Soviet system in Eastern Europe, demonstrated in the East German uprising of 1953, the Hungarian Revolution and Polish mutiny in 1956, the Czechoslovak "spring" in 1968, and the subsequent development of Solidarity in Poland and the dissident movements elsewhere. Outraged nationalism—hatred for foreign occupation and domination—powered the waves of protest in Eastern Europe in 1989 which culminated in the breaching of the Berlin Wall.

The eventual collapse of Soviet imperial power was foreseeable; indeed, inevitable. As I have argued before,* the essential failure of the Soviet Union as a superpower, an imperial power, was its inability to impose itself culturally upon its conquests, as successful empires in the past had done, those of Rome, Spain, Britain, and France. After those empires themselves had retreated, the colonial elites and populations proved to have been decisively changed. They had internalized the ideas and values of the imperial powers, even while struggling to recover national independence. The Soviet Union failed to display an equivalent cultural authority, or élan or magnetism, qualities of evident superiority and apparent inevitability able to evoke mimesis (to use Toyn-

*In two articles in *The New Yorker* magazine, on December 22, 1980, and December 26, 1988, and in newspaper columns of the period, an argument which I recapitulated in *Barbarian Sentiments* in 1989.

bee's term)—able to persuade the East Europeans that they wanted the Soviet Union as their model, wanted to follow it, would accept its values, saw in it their future.

It was otherwise in successful empires. Those conquered by Rome wanted to become Roman citizens. Elites in colonial India, Indochina, and Africa in the nineteenth and early twentieth centuries wanted to study at Oxford or in Paris. Young Indonesians went to Leiden, and made themselves scholars of the Germanic languages. The notion that a young Pole or Hungarian of the 1960s or 1970s would have longed to go to Moscow to find a place among its poets and scholars, to adopt its language and styles, imitate its fashions, study its history and literature, bear its civilization back to his own country, is patently laughable. His father and grandfather had wanted to study in Berlin or Vienna or Paris, or New York—and so did he. Nothing in the half century of Soviet occupation of Eastern Europe produced conversions to the values and ideas of the Soviet Union. The revolutionary prestige the Soviet Union had possessed among the middle-class intelligentsia and the working class before the Second World War (and continued to possess in the West, in some circles, until the 1980s) was discredited by the actual experience of Soviet occupation. The idealism of the prewar Communist movement, which had been reinforced in the selfless struggle against Nazism, and inspired many of those who set up the first postwar Communist governments in Eastern Europe, justifying for them the violence and betrayals "necessary" to save humanity from itself, rapidly became corrupted into cynicism or careerism—or turned its possessors towards dissidence, resistance, or exile.

The speed of the empire's collapse had not been so easily

80   foreseen, since Mikhail Gorbachev's logical, but radical and dangerous, decision to abandon the Soviet position in Eastern and Central Europe, and crucially in Germany itself, was unforeseeable. These were sacrifices meant to save what he considered the essential: a reformed Party rule in the Soviet Union itself, which in the event proved impossible. What began as an effort to remake the Communist system as an internally democratic, law-abiding form of one-party government actually destroyed it. Gorbachev proved to be the Aleksandr Kerensky of the new Russian revolution, the moderate overturned by the revolution's radicalization. The Transcaucasian and Asian empire which the czars had created in the eighteenth and nineteenth centuries and the Bolsheviks had taken over foundered as well. The residue of internationalist ideology was swept away, in passion and relief.

With it went the belief—proud assertion of human confidence, derived from the Enlightenment—that human affairs and human possibilities can be mastered by scientific analysis and totally submitted to rational control. The intellectual influence enjoyed for a century by Marxism and Leninism derived from their claim to provide redemptory and infallible knowledge, product of the conviction, as Engels put it, that "with the same certainty with which we can develop from given mathematical principles a new mathematical proposition, with the same certainty we can deduce from the existing economic relations and the principles of political economy the imminence of social revolution." The administration of a great state, Lenin added, once stripped of the mystifications with which capitalist power had surrounded it, could be reduced to "operations of registering, filing, and checking that . . . can easily be performed by every literate person." This proved not to be so.

The events of the *annus mirabilis* of 1989 have variously been described as the triumph of capitalism or of liberal democracy—a "victory" of the United States and the western powers in the cold war. In a sense that obviously is true, but in only a very limited sense. One of Mikhail Gorbachev's associates, Georgi Arbatov, longtime head of the Academy of Sciences' U.S.A. and Canada Institute, has said that the Reagan administration's arms spending actually delayed reform in the Soviet Union for a decade, since it strengthened conservative elements who contended that the United States was preparing a first strike on the U.S.S.R. American conservatives generally have argued the opposite, that augmented American arms programs forced Soviet reform by creating a challenge Moscow could not afford to counter.

What happened in Soviet-controlled Europe was essentially a series of profoundly nationalist upheavals against foreign oppression, by peoples who indeed wished to be prosperous, democratic, even capitalist, and to rejoin a western cultural as well as political community from which they had been barred, but who wanted first of all, and most of all, to rid themselves of Soviet occupation and the agents of Soviet occupation, to become free again to be themselves—which logically implied, of course, the possibility of their becoming again, as many of them had been in the past, not at all democratic, but authoritarian in government, intolerant of religious and ethnic difference, and aggressive towards their neighbors.

A remarkable aspect of the great liberation of 1989 was its quality as a moral victory: moral energy had inspired the forms of political and material dissidence and resistance

82   which sapped and finally destroyed Communist authority. This moral force remained a significant element in the legitimacy of the new leaders who initially dealt with the East-Central European and Balkan legacy of intolerance and conflict, as well as the moral wreckage produced by forty years of Communism. As President Václav Havel described it in his 1990 New Year's address to what then was still the Czechoslovak Republic, this was a legacy "of moral illness . . . saying one thing and thinking another . . . a sad heritage . . . we must accept . . . as something we have inflicted on ourselves." The exiled Polish poet Czeslaw Milosz was asked on a visit to Poland in 1990 what he thought people had learned from their experience of Communism, and he replied, "Resistance to stupidities." However, what soon followed in Yugoslavia demonstrated that this was not everywhere true.

It was possible to believe that this moral renewal could produce a change in national assumptions and international relationships comparable to that which emerged in Western Europe in the shaken aftermath of the Second World War, when Jean Monnet presented Germany with the French government's proposal for a common authority over France and Germany's coal and steel industries, the Schuman Plan, in 1950, the foundation upon which the European Community has since been built. In the decades since, that European Community has become what the people of Eastern Europe came to regard as "a dream, a utopia," as a Romanian intellectual, Andrei Plesu (first post-Communist minister of culture in that country), has said. But he also asked what the factors of integration would be in the future: "The consciousness of unity is stronger in Europe than anywhere else in the world. This is explained by the homogeneity of Europe in the Middle Ages, due to Christianity. This Christian Europe no longer exists. What will tie Europe together in the future? The Ecu [European currency unit]? That as solution appears to me romantic. One of the dangers is to confound unity with uniformity. Why construct a 'Europe' which is very civilized but boring?"

The question is fundamental, and in 1991 Serbian nationalists, in collaboration with extremists elsewhere in what had been Yugoslavia, gave an answer in which there was no boredom, as there was little boredom in Europe's past. The Serbians' was an answer which contradicted both what has been changed in the political relationships among the West European countries and the dimensional shift in the Europeans' consciousness of their Europe as a precious civilization whose permanence is by no means assured. Among themselves, the West Europeans had thought that they had overcome the forces of self-destruction in their society. The end of the cold war had offered a respite from external threat to the destruction of European civilization. With the war in Yugoslavia they found the internal threat broken loose again, from a country on the edge of their pacified Europe—until that moment a candidate for membership in their Europe, a place where they had gone to ski and swim, a country they had taken for granted as part of their world—whose people abruptly demonstrated to them that the terrible European past remained a part, a potential, of the European present.

4 *Hapsburg and Ottoman Internationalism*

The past lies in strata, layers of human experience, never totally forgotten even when deeply buried in a society's consciousness. "We have been waiting for this moment for eight centuries," the defense minister of newly independent Croatia said in August 1991, as his country's struggle began. These strata are layers of sophistication, of accumulated experience—even of thought. There is an important division separating those societies which have been through the "modern" experience—which means Reformation, Renaissance, Enlightenment, and Revolution—and those which have not. The division largely coincides with a religious divide, that between western Catholicism and Protestantism, progenitors of the modern West, and Orthodox Christian and Moslem Europe.

The population of Europe came from successive migrations pushing their way towards the Atlantic coast, or southwest, past the Pyrenees, into the Iberian peninsula, while many settled along the way, usually alongside earlier settlements. Prehistory still is poorly known, although there is little doubt that men essentially like modern man in looks and intelligence existed as far back as we have evidence of human settlement—men capable of extraordinary works of art and monumental construction. Nowhere in Western Europe is there a substantial community which can be said to be ethnically "pure" in any scientifically meaningful sense, and nowhere can the intermixture of human groups be said to be complete, with total assimilation of successive migrations.

In most of Western Europe these ethnic differences, which also are cultural, have become trivial, certainly non-lethal—"folkloric," as the French say. Yet they also have a political character, since the relations between groups from the very beginning were competitive and produced rivalry, feud, warfare, and the subordination or submission of one to another, and these past events are still alive in the memories of peoples. The differences between Irish and English, or Scottish and English, or Bretons, Basques, or Catalans and the Gaulish and Germanic French, or Catalans and Castilians, certainly are not trivial. However, they are manageable today within the framework of mature nation-states.

This is not the case in the east of Europe, where nations were established on the ethnic principle in the nineteenth and early twentieth centuries. Here the time lines are crucial. Bohemia and Poland are undeniably part of West European civilization and the modern world, even though they have been heavily influenced by existence at the edge of the West, on its frontier with the Byzantine, Muscovite, and Ottoman civilizations. Hungary is a western nation, Catholic and Calvinist in religion, although marked by medieval struggle with the Turks and a century and a half of Ottoman occupation. The Baltic states are also western.

86   An analyst at the French National Scientific Research Center, Krzysztof Pomian, describes the line of religious division as more like "a zone" starting

> from the north, where it passes between Finland and the Baltic Republics and Russia, crosses Byelorussia, separates Poland from Ukraine, and cuts through Romania, leaving Transylvania to the west, then descending into Yugoslavia to pass between Croatia on one side and Serbia and Bosnia-Herzegovina on the other. This line thus goes from the White Sea to the Adriatic and corresponds with the division between Latin and Greek Christianity. It is also a line of historical division. Between the twelfth and fourteenth centuries the territory north of the Dniester was controlled by the Mongols of the Golden Horde. Later, little by little, it fell into Russia's holding at the time of Russia's furthest advance in the West, after the Polish partitions. In the south, the Balkans were dominated by the Ottomans from the fourteenth century to the end of the nineteenth. During these long centuries these two regions which made up Eastern Europe were literally cut out of European history.

Today these peoples to the east express a determination to rejoin that history and become part of modern Europe. Yet this is a society they scarcely know. As nation-states, most have yet to demonstrate their ability to live by a secular political standard, juridically indifferent to the ethnic and religious identities of individual citizens. In the past the ethnic and communal multiplicity of these societies was accommodated in the essentially corporate or feudal political structures of the Ottoman and Hapsburg empires. Since those came to an end in 1918, the new ethnic nations that followed have found no lasting solution to their difficulties, which are very great. They, together with Central Europe's Jews and the peoples of the Soviet Union, bore the most ferocious

consequences of the two twentieth-century totalitarianisms,   *87*
an ordeal from which they are only now recovering.*

Nationhood of the western, secular, and ethnically plural
kind presents no inherent obstacle to democracy or to the
protection of human rights, since minorities are not, as such,
excluded from the nation, as they naturally are in the ethnically defined nation. This is what distinguishes the dominant
western model of nationhood from the new nations which
emerged from the collapse of Austria-Hungary and the Ottoman Empire. There, where political identity is connected
with ethnicity and religion, nationality and citizenship are
exclusive and cannot be compromised—or escaped. This is
an element in the dilemma of contemporary Yugoslavia,
where a significant part of the younger population is composed of the offspring of different tribes. Of those Serbs living in Croatia who married during the 1980s, 29 percent took
Croatian spouses. In Bosnia-Herzegovina, when fighting began there in 1992, 16 percent of the children were the issue of
"mixed" marriages. For whom were they supposed to fight?

If ethnic identity is the basis of nationality, others cannot be fully equal, since equality implies interchangeability.
Others are rival and potentially threatening, and since the
frontiers between national groups are often indistinct or arbitrary, with groups of different ethnic nationality intermin-
gled, there has always been invidious discrimination by
dominant groups against the aliens inside the national fron-

*One of their greatest losses was the murder or emigration of most of
their Jews. Jorge Semprum has written (in the French Jewish journal *Les
nouveaux cahiers*) that "the absence of Jewish culture in the center of Europe is one of the most preoccupying and most negative elements of our
epoch. Nothing in Central Europe today replaces that possibility of universalism, that constant transcendence of the rootedness of place."

88   tiers, with tension over the definition of borders and claims by one side or the other to enclaves of its tribe living on the far side of the tribal frontier. This was the cause of the Yugoslav War and the motive for the ethnic "cleansing" carried out in the course of that war by Serbs, Croatians, and Moslems in the regions they conquered. It has been the problem of Albanian and Hungarian minorities inside the new Serbia, the reason for the Azeri-Armenian struggle over Nagorno-Karabakh, and the cause of the conflicts involving ethnic Russian minorities in Moldova, the Baltic states, and other regions of the former Soviet Union.

The situation of the Hungarian minorities in Romania, Slovakia, and Ukraine is difficult. One third of the total number of the ethnic Hungarians of Austria-Hungary were left outside the borders of the Hungarian state created in 1920 by the Treaty of Trianon. (This was the main reason Hungary allied itself with Germany and Italy in the 1930s. Thanks to the alliance with Germany it was able to recover some of its disputed territories from Slovakia and Transylvania in 1938 and 1940—only to lose them again in 1945.) Hungarians outside Hungary even today are the largest national minority in Europe, and concern for the defense of Hungarian communities abroad was a rallying issue of the pre-1989 democratic opposition to Communism in Hungary. The number of ethnic Hungarians living in Slovakia at the start of the 1990s is put at six hundred thousand, in Serbia five hundred thousand, in Ukraine two hundred thousand. The number in Transylvania, inside Romania, is estimated to be two million. Throughout most of the region, surviving Jews and Gypsies still meet hostility and invidious discrimination, burdened by genocidal memory.

The total number of these ethnic conflicts is nonetheless smaller than before the Second World War, since during
and after that war large numbers were simply done away with
on ethnic or racial grounds. When the war was in its final
months, and during the terrible first months of peace, peoples who were minorities within states dominated by other
nationalities, or whose existence was an obstacle to the re-
drafting of ethnically exclusive new frontiers, were expedi-
tiously murdered or expelled, the latter becoming "displaced
persons," in the bureaucratic usage of the period.

When Poland was compelled by the postwar settlements
to move itself bodily westward, the unfortunate Poles native
to the territories the Poles were forced to cede to the Soviet
Union had to move westward, and the Germans in what now
was to become western Poland were ejected—those who had
not already taken to the roads with the retreating *Wehrmacht*.
East Prussia became partly Russia, partly Poland. Its capital,
Königsberg, founded in 1255 by the Teutonic Knights, who
had conquered the earlier settlers of the region, a Baltic people identified (because pagan) as "Saracens of the North,"
was renamed Kaliningrad (after M. I. Kalinin, a figure in the
October Revolution and titular head of the Soviet state from
1919 to 1946). Stalin repopulated his part of East Prussia with
something like a million people brought from Russia itself,
Belorussia (as it was then), the Ukraine, and even Kazakh-
stan. When Lithuania regained independence in 1991, ex-
Prussian Königsberg/Kaliningrad became an enclave of
Russia wedged between Lithuania and Poland, with no territorial link to Russia itself—just as, before the war, East Prussia had been a separated German territory inside Poland, and
for that reason a source of trouble and unrest.

•

These horrific wartime and postwar acts of demo-graphic surgery were imposed upon populations already very complex, the result of what the British historian Robin Okey describes as "the so-called *Völkerwanderung* or migration of peoples which followed the collapse of the Roman empire."

In the sixth and seventh centuries Slav peoples, already in-stalled in Poland, moved into Bohemia and the Balkans. But they did not entirely disperse the earlier inhabitants, particu-larly the forefathers of the modern Albanians in their west Balkan mountain fortress and the Latin-speaking Romanians north of the Danube, and they failed to withstand totally the pressure of later arrivals, like the Asiatic Magyars (or Hun-garians), who settled in the Danube basin in 896, or the Ger-mans, who pushed downwards from Bavaria through the Austrian Alps, inwards into the mountainous girdle of Slav Bohemia and eastwards from the Elbe into nascent Poland. This settlement pattern by which the Slavs came to form the majority of the population of Eastern Europe, but had to share it with a large minority of non-Slavs, was to have fateful consequences for the area. Gradually splitting up into sepa-rate groups—the east Slav Russians and Ukrainians, the west Slav Poles, Czechs and Slovaks and the south Slav Serbs, Croats, Slovenes and Bulgars (of which the last family was isolated from the others by non-Slav settlement)—the Slavic peoples lost the initiative which numbers might have given them.

Until the nineteenth century, the imperial systems to which the nations or proto-nations of East-Central, Eastern, and Balkan Europe belonged conceded them various degrees of autonomy while withholding sovereignty. This was feasi-ble, even normal, in the feudal and early modern periods, but in the eighteenth and nineteenth centuries the development of national consciousness began. A modern intelligentsia began to emerge, anxious to record and restore their distinctive histories and recall—and embellish—past glories allegedly suppressed by the imperial overlords. Out of this process came the modern nations of the region, all of them with less than a century of independent existence when Communist power was imposed on them in 1945–1949.

The larger of these empires, the Ottoman, was the creation of a Turkish people possessing a military technology and tactical capacity superior to those it encountered in its movement westward from Central Asia in the early Middle Ages (employing massed cavalry against infantry armies). The empire's expansion eventually took the Turkish army to Vienna, where in 1683, after a three-month siege of the city, it was defeated by the Polish king, John Sobieski. The Turks nonetheless remained across the Danube in Hungary for a century and a half, and at the peak of their power also incorporated (in Europe) the territories of modern Greece, Bulgaria, Romania (Moldavia and Walachia), Serbia, Albania, Bosnia-Herzegovina, and Macedonia, holding all of them until the nineteenth or early twentieth centuries. (They also dominated the Middle East and the southern Mediterranean coast.)

Of these states, Serbia, Bulgaria, Moldavia, and Walachia had enjoyed a period of national existence in the Middle Ages. Serbia was the first to rise against the Turks in modern times, in 1804. Greece was next to rebel, in 1821 ("I dreamed that Greece might yet be free"—thus Byron, the English poet, who died there). Bulgaria and Romania were detached from Turkish control in the nineteenth century under pressure from Russia, which made itself protector of their Ortho-

92   dox populations, expecting to dominate them, which in the Bulgarian case it has mostly done ever since. On the other hand, Moldavia, or a part of it, remained in contention between Moscow and Bucharest. Those Moldavians who in 1940 were annexed by the Soviet Union, and subjected to a forced Russification, compelled to write their Romance language in Cyrillic characters, in 1992 declared independence as Moldova, resumed the Latin alphabet of their fellow Moldavians across the Prut River—and turned on the Russian minority installed in their country, who then had to look to Moscow for support. Thus does a suspended history resume.

The Ottoman Empire was politically corporatist, identifying its many separate "nations" or communities by ethnic origin, communal tradition or history, or religion. The Oxford historian Albert Hourani speaks of the non-Moslem as well as Moslem political entities of the empire as including towns, villages, pastoral tribes, city neighborhoods or quarters, and trades and crafts organized in institutions resembling the guilds of medieval Europe. Christians and Jews were allowed their religious law and the free exercise of religion, as well as their own schools and hospitals. The Turkish authorities granted a certain legal jurisdiction to the head of each community as well as holding him accountable for the community's good order and its taxation. Hourani goes on: "In this way, the non-Moslems were integrated into the body politic. They did not fully belong to it but an individual might rise to a position of power and influence. . . . They do not seem to have lived in isolation or under pressure . . . worship and education were free within limits. They could carry on most economic activities: Jews were important as bankers, Greeks in the sea-trade, and by the sixteenth century Arme-

nians were beginning to be important in the trade in Armenian silk."

Jewish, Christian, and Druze communities of the empire had quasi-autonomous status, and the members of each
community were dealt with politically as members of their
group, the authorities acting through a recognized leader of
the group. In some respects theirs was an invidious status; for
example, they had to pay a form of personal tax from which
the Moslem citizens of the empire were exempt. In exchange,
until nearly the end of the Ottoman period, they were excluded from military service. In 1910, when the Ottoman
Empire's decline in Europe was already advanced, it was estimated (by the contemporary edition of the *Encyclopaedia Britannica*) to be only 50 percent Moslem in population. It was
41 percent Orthodox Christian and 6 percent Catholic; all
other non-Moslems—Christians (Nestorians), Druze, and
Jews—made up 3 percent of the population. This meant that
in the European provinces some two thirds of the population
was Christian. In the Asiatic part of the empire there was estimated to be a population of somewhat more than thirteen
million people, of whom there were ten million Moslems,
some three million Christians, a quarter-million Jews, somewhat more than a quarter-million Druze, and some two hundred thousand Gypsies. The non-Moslem communities
legally recognized in 1910 were Latin, Maronite, and Armenian Roman Catholics; Greek Orthodox; Armenian Gregori-
ans; Syrian and Chaldean Orthodox Christians; Protestants;
and Jews.

The Ottoman system in the early nineteenth century was
the largest of all modern state systems, while not being modern at all. The ruler was not an individual but a family, the
House of Osman, and succession was within the family but

94   according to no rigid rule. The head of government was an official appointed by the family, the grand vizier, who was given absolute power. He acted through secretaries and councils of lesser officials, and through governors he appointed over cities and regions, all with their own households, secretaries, and councils. Patronage was very important. Members of the imperial household were "slaves" of the sultan whether they were actual slaves or not (although many, descendants of conquered peoples, were).

Hourani writes:

> The organization and modes of activity of the government reflected that Persian ideal of kingship which [held that the] . . . just and wise ruler should stand apart from the different orders of society to enable him to regulate their activities and maintain the harmony of the whole. . . . This separation was shown in the life of the ruler, secluded in the inner courts of his Topkapi palace on a hill overlooking the Bosphorus, living among his slaves and *harim*, never—after the reign of Suleyman (1520–66)—contracting marriages with Ottoman families which might in this way be given too much influence. It was expressed too in the existence of a court culture: a refined code of manners, an Ottoman Turkish language enriched by borrowings from Persian as well as Arabic, an education which included the polite literature of Persian as well as the religious literature of Arabic.

The system demanded of its subjects obedience, tribute, and taxes, but not ideological conformity, religious conversion, or social conformation to the model of the governing power. This was to prove a weakness later, but for a long time it allowed the Ottomans to exercise arbitrary but also relatively undemanding power. The empire was open to the social and political ascension of the conquered and the governed, offering the *carrière ouverte aux talents*. It was, in short, a system close to the empires of antiquity, and quite incapable of dealing either with the modern European nations which in the eighteenth and nineteenth centuries began picking it apart, or with the force of modern nationalism inside the European part of the empire, and eventually in Arabia.

The Ottoman breakdown in the nineteenth and early twentieth centuries was thus a phenomenon of its inadaptability, an institutional loss of ability to accommodate communal tensions as they assumed the new forms produced by literacy, the growth of the educated class, and the influence of political and intellectual currents from the West. The Ottomans nonetheless had dominated their "internal" nations more successfully, and for a much longer period, than the Hapsburg emperors did theirs.

Each of the proto-nations in the Ottoman system— Walachia and Moldavia (of Dacian, non-Slav origin); non-Slav (Magyar) Hungary, Greece, and Albania; Bulgaria and Serbia—had acquired a distinct political identity in the early Middle Ages under dynastic chieftains and kings. This occurred in Hungary in the tenth century, and in Serbia and Bulgaria in the ninth to fourteenth centuries (before these two fell under particularly oppressive forms of Ottoman domination). Walachia and Moldavia formed self-governing principalities under Ottoman suzerainty from the fourteenth century on. Albania's existence was essentially tribal in political character until the early twentieth century (when in its haste to make itself a modern nation, its throne was twice offered to the British traveler and sometime spy Aubrey Herbert, son of the fourth Earl of Carnarvon and model for the hero of John Buchan's *Greenmantle*).

The awakening of national cultural consciousness in the nineteenth century took place mainly under West European influences. A. J. P. Taylor writes: "The first age of national awakening is strictly academic. It is led by university professors and is concerned with such things as the study of medieval manuscripts, the evolution of a national language from a peasant dialect, and the rewriting of history on national lines. The second stage comes when the pupils of the professors get out into the world."

Serbia's national struggle began with an uprising which freed the province of Belgrade in 1804; the Serbs obtained autonomy, thanks to Russian support and protection, in 1829. Greece's rebellion in 1821 took place under the influence of the French Revolution and Turkish reverses in the Russo-Turkish wars, and with the help of West European volunteers.

The first modern work in the Bulgarian language was published in 1762, although political rebellion did not come until 1876, resulting eventually in Bulgaria's liberation by Russia (which anticipated dominating the new state, and has in fact done so for most of the period since). Moldavia and Walachia—under Mongol rule for a period in the thirteenth century, and thereafter Ottoman vassal states—were after the eighteenth century under direct Ottoman control through Greek governors, resulting in landlord rule and serfdom. The national movement which followed also enjoyed Russian support and was directed primarily against the Greek elite, ending with the recognition of the two Romanian states by the Sublime Porte as Russian protectorates. (The "sublime" gate or door opened into the offices of the grand vizier, supreme power in the empire.) Walachia and Moldavia united in the 1860s and invited the Hohenzollern-Sigmaringen Carol I, a Prussian army officer, to become their monarch.

The Ottoman Empire's Christian provinces thus were mostly lost in the nineteenth century, under particular pressure from the Russian government, which was ostensibly concerned with the protection of Orthodox communities but was also ambitious to expand Russian influence. Greece, Bulgaria, Montenegro, Serbia, and Romania all became independent before the end of the century. Turkey by then, in the metaphor of the period, was the Sick Man of Europe, incapable of a creative response to its troubles, or of making a serious political defense against the foreign powers now taking it apart. Bosnia and Herzegovina were handed over to Austrian administration, and Cyprus to Britain. International pressures forced measures of reform in Armenia and Crete.

The Young Turk "revolution" of 1908 was the first step towards formation of a homogeneous Turkish nation, although it was intended simply to reform the polyglot imperial system. Secular government was imposed. However, this added to the unrest which already existed, not only among the Christian Ottoman populations but in Moslem Albania, Yemen (another ancient nation, like Mesopotamia and Egypt), and Arabia itself, where the Bedouin custodian of the Holy Places, Husayn, sharif of Mecca, was to ally himself in 1916 with Britain to launch the "Arab Revolt." Auxiliary to the British army's attack on Turkish holdings throughout the eastern Mediterranean, this resulted in the ejection of Ottoman power from the Arabian peninsula and Palestine, Syria, and Iraq (the last also attacked by forces from British India).

98   Before the war, the Young Turks had themselves sought a European protector and sponsor, but were turned down by Britain, France, and even Russia. When the war broke out, Turkey became a belligerent through a series of events that included much misunderstanding on all sides as well as British policy blunders (as David Fromkin tells it in his account of the Ottoman collapse, *A Peace to End All Peace*). The Turks had wanted to stay out of the war, but despite themselves became allies of Germany and Austria, and were eventually defeated—even though they did not do badly in the European theater of their war. Against Russia they were very successful, and as Russian forces faded away following the February Revolution in 1917 and the installation of the Provisional Government in Petrograd, the Turks successfully attacked Georgia, Armenia, and Azerbaijan, and approached the oil-producing center of Baku. However, Germany's failure on the western front forced the Turks to seek an armistice, which proved a surrender. Thus did the six-century Ottoman experiment in the corporate government of disparate and often hostile communities come to an end.

In the feudal Christian Roman Empire, the reciprocal relationships of power and obligation between emperor and pope had left secular authority to be exercised by the emperor with the acquiescence of the pope, the spiritual ruler and God's vicar. In practice, this meant a duality of power and the legitimation of secular government, whose authority was acknowledged supreme in its own realm. Nothing like this occurred in the eastern Byzantine Empire, or in Islam, a fact with effect ever since in the difficulties East European, Russian, and Islamic societies have encountered in establishing lasting and capable secular governments.

The complicated multinationality of the Hapsburg Empire was a relatively late development in what, at the beginning, was merely one of the considerable number of German principalities making up the Holy Roman Empire. Austria—*Österreich* in German, which is to say "the eastern realm"—was a buffer state defending the Danube frontier of the empire against the Slavs and Magyars. Its Hapsburg rulers expanded the realm by battle, dynastic hazard, and marriage. ("Let others wage war," it was said in the late fifteenth century; "thou, happy Austria, marry.") From the fifteenth century on, with a single exception, the Holy Roman Empire's electors gave the imperial title to a Hapsburg. Marriage into the Burgundian and Spanish courts extended Hapsburg holdings into France, Spain, and the Low Countries. Later, the Austrian monarchy acquired the crowns of Bohemia and Hungary, and participated in the partition of Poland. After the Turks' defeat at Vienna in 1683, and the campaigns across the Danube which allowed Austria to retake Hungary and territories beyond, Vienna, which until then still was merely one among several German capital cities, became the intellectual and artistic center of South-Central Europe, and Austria became a European great power. However, the Hapsburgs' incorporation of all or part of three major non-German historical nations, which never were wholly reconciled to their position in a German-dominated system, was crucial to the Hapsburg system's eventual weakening and to the rise of Prussia. Hungary, Bohemia, and Poland all were important nations of medieval Central Europe—indeed, at the time, more important than Austria itself.

In the nineteenth century the Hapsburg system included Germans, Hungarians, Czechs, Poles, Slovaks, Ruthenes (of

100   Carpathian Ruthenia, part of Russia since 1945), Italians, Serbs, Slovenes, Croatians, and still others. But in 1866 Bismarck deliberately provoked the Seven Weeks' War in order to drive Austria out of the German Confederation (successor to the empire; the Hapsburg monarch had renounced the Holy Roman Emperor's title during the Napoleonic Wars). The new-model Prussian professional army made short work of Austria's forces, and Prussia became the new German great power, its capital Berlin. Hapsburg Austria, which at the beginning of the nineteenth century had been the principal member of a large, loose, quasi-feudal association of mainly German states, was left the German member of a multinational and multiconfessional empire in which the eight million German Austrians were a minority.

    The national demands of the Hungarians brought about the so-called 1867 Compromise creating a dual monarchy, two quasi-autonomous states under the Hapsburg crown. Hungary was given home rule, a parliament (soon housed in a Danubian replica of Britain's Houses of Parliament), its own cabinet and civil administration, and the use of Hungarian as an official language. However, the negative consequence of this was the impetus given to the national claims of Croatians, Czechs, Poles, Slovenes, Ruthenians, the Serbs who lived inside the empire, and all the other national minorities. Most of these were within Hungary's frontiers. Hungary at the time included nearly as many non–ethnic Hungarians as Hungarians; the official statistic in 1900 showed a 51.4 percent Magyar majority. This was the result of migrations and settlements subsequent to the Magyar arrival in the region, as well as of the relatively low birthrate of the Magyars themselves. Giving Hungary equal power and

standing with Austria in the empire confirmed the invidious
inferiority of all the rest.

There was no real rationale for Hapsburg Vienna's rule
over the others (nor that of Vienna plus Budapest). Feudal
obligation, God's empire, the divine right of monarchy, all
had been justifications of the system in the past, but these no
longer worked in the late nineteenth and early twentieth centuries. The nationalities demanded to rule themselves. A
year after the 1867 Compromise, a form of Croatian autonomy had to be conceded by Hungary. However, as this was
not equality, Croatian resentment was stoked. The other nationalities were not even granted universal male suffrage—
nor were the Hungarians willing to yield it. The next-to-last
Hapsburg emperor, Francis Joseph—nostalgically recalled in
ex-Hapsburg Europe today   was actually a dispirited reactionary unable to deal with the rising nationalisms in his
realm and incapable of an ideological justification for his
own continued possession of hereditary power a century after the French Revolution, in a society well advanced into the
industrial revolution. A. J. P. Taylor writes:

His only thought was of dynastic power. Yet, though rigid in
his dynastic aims, he was ready to try any means of sustaining
his Empire. He began with military dictatorship and sometimes reverted to it. Taught by defeat, he made concessions
to all in turn; the Compromise of 1867 gave Hungary internal independence, and in the same year Austria received a
liberal Constitution. Later he sought to win over the Czechs,
and finally, in 1907, forced universal suffrage through the
Austrian parliament in order to be able to play off the masses
against the middle-class politicians in a vast game of *rouge et
noir*. His greatest hatred was for "liberalism"—the attempt to

102   limit the prerogatives of the Crown. Against this liberalism
he would call on any ally and would even invoke the rival nationalisms which were tearing his Empire to pieces.

The assassination at Sarajevo of the emperor's nephew,
Francis Ferdinand, and of the latter's wife, was an act of Ser-
bian-sponsored terrorism, meant to serve the cause of Ser-
bian-dominated pan-Slavism. Austria-Hungary held Serbia
accountable; Serbia had Russia's support; France was Russia's
ally; Germany was Austria's ally—and Germany's rigid war
planning required it to strike France first, to defeat it before
turning to the less urgent threat from Russia's armies. The
sinister sequence of events is well known. The world war thus
set off, which, of course, no Austrian official (or Serb) had
anticipated, was far beyond the Hapsburg system's capacity
to survive. The war brought down the existing European order, and prepared the bloody ground for the twentieth century's totalitarianisms and racial wars. "Injuries were
wrought to the structure of human society which a century
will not efface," Winston Churchill wrote afterwards, and he
was right.

The Hapsburg and Ottoman systems each provided
ways to accommodate individual nationhood—ethnic and religious communities, but also historical nations—within a
larger political authority. Both failed in 1918. The failures are
not entirely to be explained in terms of discrepancies in historical maturity on some arguable scale of political development, although the Ottoman system had remained in
essential respects premodern, its semi-nomadic origin influencing its political character to the end. The Hapsburg system was also never freed from an absolutism impossible to

maintain in the face of the rise of the middle classes, mass literacy, and the loss of power by the peasantry, whose implicit
alliance with the aristocracy—they were the two so-called
Austrian classes—offset the power of the urban populations.
Institutional incompetence was a factor in the failure of
both. However, nationalism was the most powerful disruptive
force, above all in the Hapsburg case: Hungary, Poland,
Croatia, Bohemia, and the Italian possessions of the empire
all were sophisticated societies possessing clear historical
identities. The final blow was administered by German nationalism—that of the Austrian Germans. Early in the world
war, at Easter 1915, all of Austria's German parties except the
Social Democrats issued a demand that Austria become a
unitary German state.

It is possible to argue that Austria-Hungary need not
have collapsed. Neither the United States, England, nor
France wished it destroyed, nor did the Croatians and Slovaks, who were endangered by Italian and Magyar claims.
The Czechs, before the war, had wanted to keep the monarchy and reform it as a federal institution. When the war and
Austrian defeats drew Vienna into an increasingly powerless
subservience to the German High Command, the Czechs,
under Tomáš Masaryk, concluded that they had to have their
independence, and to be plausible needed to take the Slovaks
along with them. By 1917 Masaryk had convinced the Allies
to make the "liberation" of Czechoslovakia a war aim. In January 1918 the Czechs demanded of Vienna a sovereign state
incorporating Slovakia (a land which had never been a
state—although it became one in July 1992). The monarchy
had no response. The Emperor Francis Joseph's successor,
Charles, was attempting to negotiate an escape from the war,
but he commanded neither his army nor his economy. By

104   that time Germany did. In October 1918 Austria capitulated
to the Allies. The empire fell apart of itself. Czechoslovakia,
Poland, Hungary, and the South Slavs all proclaimed their
independence. The German members of the *Reichsrat* proclaimed "German-Austria." The army broke into national
units. The resemblance to events in the ex-U.S.S.R. during
1991–1992 is close. Charles refused to abdicate, but departed,
leaving Austria, and the disposal of his realm, to the Allies.

Some of the nationalities of the old empire would today
like nothing better than to be reintegrated into a successor to
the Hapsburg system. The heir, Otto von Hapsburg, a European Parliament deputy, was enthusiastically, even tearfully,
cheered when he returned to Budapest after the fall of Communism, to address the Hungarian Parliament in splendid
Hungarian. The former Hapsburg nations today urgently
press their candidacies for membership in the European
Community, the new expression of a lost European universalism. But this new universalism is not linked to German
Europe, like that of the Hapsburgs, but to an earlier period
of Christian universalism when, as Zamoyski has written,
Polish Lutherans took for granted that their sons would
study at Wittenberg, and Polish Calvinists in Basel, while
Catholics went to Italy.

That was a Europe where Romanesque churches were
built from central Norway and Kirkwall in the Orkneys to
Palermo in Sicily, and from Santiago on the Spanish Atlantic
coast to Kraków; and Italian architects designed the monu-
mental buildings of Prague and Leningrad as well as those of
Dresden and Paris. It was a Europe where Charlemagne had
Italian and Spanish as well as German and French advisers.
The re-creation of this universalism was the moral purpose

of the Franco-German reconciliation solemnly confirmed at
Konrad Adenauer and Charles de Gaulle's meeting in the
Cathedral of Reims in 1962. The new European universalism
is superficially a matter of economic and political integration, but its most important element is the attempt to re-
assert this cultural unity. In Western Europe this has been a
success. However, the ambition (one cannot yet call it a substantial effort) to incorporate, or reincorporate, what in the
past was Byzantine and Moslem Europe has as yet been a failure, with ominous implications for what is to come.

The eighteenth century and the French Revolution produced the modern nation-state, and it was then that states
began to justify themselves as the political manifestations of
defined peoples previously submerged and now liberated (or
in need of liberation) from alien domination. The peace settlements which followed the First World War, the treaties of
Saint-Germain, Neuilly, Trianon, and Sèvres, legitimated
these claims, following the argument, promoted by the
American government, that peoples must themselves be allowed to choose the sovereignties under which they are to
live. The lack of realism in American war aims, as George
Kennan has written, caused Woodrow Wilson to go to Europe in 1919 "unprepared to face the sordid but all-important
details of the day of reckoning. Under this theory he suffered
his tragic and historical failure." His was "the colossal con-
ceit of thinking that you could suddenly make international
life over into what you believed to be your own image; when
you dismissed the past with contempt, rejected the relevance
of the past to the future, and refused to occupy yourself with
the real problems that a study of the past would suggest."
The theory held that Hapsburg and Ottoman Europe

106 should be reconstructed on the basis of ethnic nationhood, although it also argued that these new nations could be less than sovereign, part of some democratic successor system to that of the Hapsburgs. Accordingly, new borders were drafted for the countries of Central, Eastern, and Balkan Europe by the young American journalist Walter Lippmann, together with four other members of a secret committee set up by President Wilson in October 1917 (called "the Inquiry"). In his biography of Lippmann, Ronald Steel writes that the five, working "from maps and piles of statistics, attacked the question of frontiers by drawing up charts showing the concentration of national groups within Europe. Lippmann then coordinated these charts and lists with national political movements to determine how these ethnic entities could be granted self-determination without triggering new European rivalries. Then he correlated this blueprint with the secret treaties [concerning the spoils of victory which the Allies had signed prior to America's entry into the war]—deciding which territorial changes were acceptable and which defied justice and logic." (The other members of this group were Sidney Mezes, president of City College of New York, a philosopher of religion, and the brother-in-law of President Wilson's adviser on international affairs, Colonel Edward M. House; David Hunter Miller, a New York law partner of Colonel House's son-in-law; James T. Shotwell, a Columbia University historian; and Isaiah Bowman, director of the American Geographical Society.) It was chiefly pressure from Czech, Slovak, and other émigré groups in the Allied countries and particularly the United States that persuaded Wilson that the de facto dismemberment of the Austro-Hungarian Empire which took place at the war's end should be made permanent in the postwar set-

tlements by the creation of new sovereignties.

The result was a group of new states defined by ethnic identity while actually incorporating minorities of other ethnic groups. The grievances of these were later to be exploited by outside powers, decisively so by Hitler's Germany, in the run-up to the Second World War. Taylor says:

despite the invocation of "self-determination," neither Poland nor Romania was a true national state: the Poles were rather less than two thirds of Poland, the Romanians rather more than two thirds of Romania. The Poles and Romanians were the "people of state" on the Hungarian model; the other nationalities, as in old Hungary, possessed only minority rights, which, as in Hungary, they were unable to exercise. . . . Czechoslovakia and Yugoslavia, the two new states, both claimed to be based on nationalism and to have found in it the uniting principles which the Hapsburg Monarchy had lacked. The Czechs and Slovaks would become one people, as the Piedmontese and Neapolitans had become Italian; Serbs, Croats, and Slovenes would merge into Yugoslavia, as Prussians, Saxons, and Bavarians had merged into Germany. The analogy was near; not near enough to prove true.

The consequences of the failure are with us in the 1990s. The ethnic character of all these states has set them apart from the old nations of Western Europe as well as the overseas nations created from West European stock: the United States, Canada, Australia, New Zealand, Argentina, Chile, and the others. It sets them off as well from the other category of "new" nations, those created after the Second World War from the old civilizations of Asia after their release from colonial bondage, and those established in Africa in the 1950s and 1960s.

•

108   Yet the situation in the former Hapsburg and Ottoman territories in the 1990s is not like that of either 1914 or 1938. There is a fundamental interest now, among all of the neighboring states and the democracies as a whole, in heading off ethnic conflict and ethnic war and forcing negotiation upon the parties. Nothing like this happened in 1914. Intervention failed in the Yugoslav case, but it is possible to believe that this failure will be taken as a lesson, although this remains to be seen. In 1914 war itself was considered an unexceptionable instrument of policy and a natural phenomenon in the Darwinian struggle of nations. Balkan conflict was unhesitatingly exploited for the aggrandizement of the great powers—considered a proper and moral goal of policy. In 1939 war was valued by the Fascist powers as an assertion and validation of national greatness. There has, since then, been a profound change in Europe, in the assumptions of national action and purpose.

5 *The Ottoman Aftermath*

T he West's domination of the world in modern times, exercised through commerce and technological superiority as well as by imperial expansion, disguises from us the scale and continuity of non-western civilization. Asia, except for Japan, has been eclipsed in modern times as an active agent of change. The return of Asia would signal an end to our world as it has existed since the sixteenth century, when Europe's imperial expansion began. The agency by which that return has been attempted is called Asian nationalism. However, this is not a nationalism which resembles that of nineteenth-century Europe. It incorporates much broader social and political forces generated by the cultural as well as political subordination of the great Asian civilizations to the West. In the Mediterranean region this developed as a consequence of the Ottoman Empire's collapse in 1918. The result was creation of a group of Middle Eastern states ruled by the European great powers by way of League of Nations mandates. There already were several nominally sovereign Moslem states actually within western spheres of imperial interest. The latter was the case   *109*

110   for Persia, Egypt, and Morocco, for example.

In East Asia in the early twentieth century the only major independent powers were Japan and China, and China was not totally in control of its own affairs until the Communists came to power in 1949. The rest of Asia, Thailand (Siam) aside, like the Middle East, was directly or indirectly dominated by the European imperial powers or by the United States. Historically speaking, this was an exceptional condition for these societies, which as political entities are not only much older than the western nations but for the greater part of their histories were also more powerful than the West. Whether they will ever become so again is an unsettled question.

The evidence of civilization exists in the urban settlements in Mesopotamia and Egypt in the fourth millennium before Christ, or possibly even before. These communities expanded out of the river valleys where they began, eventually meeting one another and encountering conflicts of interest and authority. In the sixth century B.C. the plateau people of Persia, under the emperor Cyrus, conquered Mesopotamia, and Cyrus' heirs conquered Egypt. Persia in its turn was challenged by the Greek alliance of free city-states, which under the Macedonian Alexander conquered Persia and much else. Rome succeeded Greece; and the sack of Rome by "barbarians" in 410 may be said to have completed a cycle of imperial successions which had begun some five thousand years earlier.

It is a failure of imagination not to recognize the temporality of western civilization, which is dwarfed in time by what preceded it (not to speak about American civilization, which is a flash in time's pan). We are a mere fifteen hundred years from the fall of Rome, and modern times have scarcely begun, although we already talk about a postmodern period. If we consider our own age in a Mesopotamian or Egyptian perspective, the efforts of Washington or Paris to influence the modern Middle East must seem trivial and ephemeral interferences into the millennial flow of civilization in these valleys where western civilization originated. But Arab nationalism, the supposed twentieth-century political agency of this civilization, is even more recent, and will undoubtedly prove more ephemeral.

There is no Arab nation, as such. The historical experience and reference of the region is not to nation but to religion, commune, empire, caliphate. The states which exist there today do so because it is now considered appropriate that people live in nation-states, not in multiconfessional and multinational empires. The Ottoman system failed to respond to the changes brought about by literacy and the evolution of communications, administration, and political organization in the modern West. In the nineteenth and twentieth centuries the western nation-state made itself by far the most successful form of political and economic organization for industrial development, and this example deeply influenced elites elsewhere. But simple imitation of the western model does not make a nation. There still are not many real nations in the Middle or Near East. Egypt, Iraq, Turkey, Iran (Persia), Yemen—and Israel—possess the social and historical credentials of nationhood. The other Eastern Mediterranean states are artificial.

Until the end of the Ottoman system in 1918, the Middle and Near East, other than Persia, had experienced only empires. The civilization of the region had developed from

112 god-king-ruled city-states that expanded outward, abhorred exclusion, and incorporated what they met. The contemporary instabilities of the region occur precisely at those fault lines where real "nations," former imperial powers, abut zones of historical non-nationhood, which in the Gulf and Eastern Mediterranean means most of the Arabian peninsula and what now is Syria, Jordan, and Israel.

It may seem odd to describe as largely nationless a region where determined, even aggressive, modern states exist, and the political forces driving events employ the language of nationalism and national liberation. However, these states are unachieved as nations; they lack historical roots, national integrity. None is more than seventy years old. Each is vulnerable. Kuwait, whose invasion by Iraq triggered war between Iraq and the West (and a fraction of the East) in 1991, exists because of an agreement made between an agent of the British government of India and an Arab chieftain at the beginning of the nineteenth century, a result of the British policy obsession of the period, which was to control the lines of imperial communication to India. The Sabah abu Abdullah family wished protection against the exactions of Ottoman imperial authorities, nominally sovereign over Kuwait. Kuwait's economy at the time rested on the pearl and hide trades.

Israel exists where Jewish kingdoms existed in antiquity, but is itself a product of secular energies and of that Romantic nineteenth-century European nationalism which said that every people should have a state. Theodor Herzl was a Hungarian journalist appalled by the anti-Semitism revealed in France by the Dreyfus affair, which he covered as correspondent for a Vienna newspaper. His pamphlet, *Der Judenstaat*, which argued that Jews should have their own state, inspired a movement which was given a terrible momentum in the

mid-twentieth century by the Nazis' attempt to exterminate
European Jewry. Zionism became a military as well as political campaign to establish that Jewish state against the opposition of both Arabs and the British government (the trustee of mandated Palestine under the League of Nations).

However, in 1948 not only a state but a nation came into existence, a Jewish nation reconstituted from the Jewish diaspora, located in a place where those in occupation, the Palestinians, were not a historical nation but members of an imperial civilization and "Arab nation." One of the consequences of the struggle between the Palestinians and the Jews which then began was the creation, in diaspora, of the Palestinian nation, which did not exist before. A second and indirect consequence was the near-mortal wounding of a Christian Lebanese nation which had existed since before Islam and the Arab conquests of the seventh century.

Palestine, together with modern Syria, Jordan, and Lebanon, and parts of what now are western Iraq and northern Saudi Arabia, composed what in the Ottoman period, and earlier, was known as Syria. For millennia this Syria had been politically fragmented, the object of repeated invasions and conquests because of its fertility and command of trade routes. Local political power was dispersed and contested, even under the more than three centuries of Ottoman rule. The only major indigenous culture of the region was the Phoenician, in the second millennium before Christ, in what now is Lebanon. The only "nation" was Christian Lebanon—predominantly Roman Catholic, practicing the ancient Maronite rite derived from Antioch. None of the other religious minority communities in Syria—the Druze (a sect of Islamic origins), Kurds, Armenians, Turkomans, Orthodox Christians, and the Islamic minorities—possessed

114   the numbers and staying power to impose itself in modern times as a nation.

After 1918, the several states formally established in the postwar agreements included Syria and Lebanon, which were given their modern frontiers and made French mandates under the League of Nations. Iraq and Transjordan (subsequently the Hashemite Kingdom of Jordan) became monarchies under British mandate. Palestine remained under direct British rule as a mandated territory. Each has a distinguishable social, historical, or linguistic character, but of the new states it is chiefly Iraq, heir to the Mesopotamian civilization, which had the credentials of nationhood. Saudi Arabia had no international political identity at all until 1932, when the present kingdom was established by the Wahhabi (a puritanical Moslem sect), whose leader, Ibn Sa'ud, had wrested control of the region from several other bedouin territorial chieftains, including Hussein, king of the Hejaz and protector of the Holy Places. Hussein's son Faisal had led the Arab revolt (T. E. Lawrence his military counselor) and was made king of Iraq in the postwar settlements. His brother Abdullah became king of Transjordan. Abdullah's grandson is the present King Hussein of Jordan. After the Second World War all these states became sovereign except Palestine, which because of the war between the Arabs and the Jews was forcibly partitioned (the UN would have partitioned it peacefully). The larger part became the state of Israel.

Iraq has a serious claim to national identity and national autonomy because the modern state exists in historical continuity with a distinct and formidable past reaching to the Mesolithic age, more than ten thousand years ago, when the earliest evidence exists of agriculture, hence of civilization. The first distinct culture zones of early Neolithic or Chalcolithic life, six millennia ago, are those in northern Mesopotamia and Syria, Palestine, and Anatolia, earlier even than those in the Nile Valley. In the fourth millennium B.C. in Mesopotamia there were villages and towns, and the beginnings of urban life, meaning specialization of labor; pooled surpluses; full-time craftsmen; professions; the invention, by the inhabitants of southern Mesopotamia, of writing, and probably of the wheel as well; and the discovery and use of bronze. The civilizations that subsequently succeeded one another here include the Sumerian, Akkadian, Babylonian, and Assyrian. (One of the Iraqi dictator Saddam Hussein's ambitions in the 1980s was to re-create the hanging gardens of Babylon.) The common western notion of Iraqis and other Arabs as backward and unsophisticated peoples is a verdict on their relative lack of industrial and technological development, by comparison with Europe and the United States. By other standards Americans and Europeans are the parvenus.

The Ottoman Empire from which these modern Eastern Mediterranean states came was the successor to the early-medieval Arab sharifian empire, or empires. The Osmanlis, a Turkish tribe migrating from Central Asia, had settled on the frontier of the Christian Byzantine Empire.* It

---

*The Central Asian societies from which these migrations came, colonized by Russia's czars and later by the Bolsheviks, are once again free. Their relative weakness and geographical remoteness mean that they remain fairly minor factors in geopolitics. However, their return to autonomous existence is worth attention. Turkey has certainly taken notice, and practices an active cultural relations and economic assistance policy in the region. Islamic fundamentalist missionaries are also present, although after eighty years of aggressive Bolshevik secularism and atheist education their possibilities for success remain problematical.

116 was one of several such Turkish settlements, and absorbed the others over a period of centuries, then beginning to move against the decaying Byzantine system, taking over several of its Balkan holdings and eventually laying siege to Constantinople itself, which fell in 1453. In the sixteenth century the Ottomans annexed Syria and Egypt and emerged as the new Islamic "universal empire," more powerful than the Umayyad and Abbasid caliphates before them, and in the early modern period more powerful than any of the European nations or empires—and seen by the latter as a mortal threat.

Empires are not nations. They incorporate nations and have expanding (or shrinking) frontiers. They include rather than exclude, as nations do. They are suitable political vehicles for religious civilizations. However, the modern world demands nations. The nations that exist today in the Middle East are all provisional, not only because they were the creations of the British and French who ran the Middle Eastern peace settlements of 1918–1923, but also because in the opinion of many Arabs there is supposed to be an "Arab nation" without internal frontiers. The rulers, at this writing, of Iraq and Syria, Saddam Hussein and Hafiz Assad, are products of the most important modern effort to bring this Arab nation into existence. The Ba'ath (Resurrection) party (one wing of which came to rule Iraq, while the other, a rival, ruled Syria) was meant to be a modern (for the time, the 1920s), "nationalist," socialist (meaning concerned with social justice), and secular political movement drawing all of the Arabs together into a modern nation-state. Unsurprisingly, this party was the creation of French-educated Christian and other minority Arabs—Druze, Alawis—in Lebanon and Syria. The idea

of an Arab nation which would be defined by its language and   *117*
history rather than by religion promised personal legitimation to them in a society to which they unmistakably belonged but from which they were excluded by religion. A
footnote to this, a note of irony in what subsequently was to
happen to western relations with the Arab world, is that this
program for an Arab nation was greatly influenced by the example of the United States. The Syrian Protestant College,
now the American University of Beirut, and the Jesuit Saint
Joseph's University in Beirut had since the mid-nineteenth
century conveyed to their students western ideas of the non-
confessional democratic state.

Islamic modernizers have mainly succeeded in producing political movements like the Ba'ath, secular in nature,
rather than reform of Islam itself, and of its relationship to
modern industrial civilization. Most successful of the national "revivals" was that of Turkey under Mustafa Kemal
(Atatürk). In the aftermath of the Ottoman collapse, he set
out to break the cultural continuity of Turkish society so as
to modernize it, banning Arabic script and Moslem practices. Religious law and religious schools were abolished.
This ruthless secularization resembled what the Bolsheviks
were doing in the neighboring Moslem regions of the Russian Empire. Turkey today no longer is the aggressively secular state it was then—an active Islamic fundamentalist
influence has developed there—but it remains a secular republican nation with functioning, if imperfect, democratic
institutions. So is Egypt, which after the Second World War
was responsible for the principal, and ephemerally successful, Arab nationalist movement, that of Colonel Gamal Abdel Nasser, who took power from the decadent monarchy in

118   1952–1953, and subsequently ejected the British and seized
the Suez Canal. He was the first of several remarkable Egyptian leaders.

   Reza Khan, another soldier, tried in the 1930s to do for
Iran what Atatürk had done in Turkey. He also fought the religious establishment and attempted to form a secular (and
authoritarian) political culture. He too emphasized the pre-
Islamic past of Persian empire. His son, Muhammad Reza
Pahlavi, deposed in 1979, attempted to continue his father's
effort but became the victim of political (and personal) pre-
tensions (encouraged by his American allies) that over-
reached his means, and of a revival of fundamentalist religion
in Iran and elsewhere that was the product of a crisis in Islam's religious as well political culture.

   The immediate occasion of that crisis was the installation
by force of Israel, an essentially European state (Ashkenazi;
Israel's Sephardic population mostly arrived later), in the
Holy Land, where the Islamic peoples had dominated since
Saladin's defeat of the Latin kingdom of Jerusalem in 1187.
The Palestinians displaced to make way for Israel afterwards
looked for revenge. This effort radicalized Arab politics, rein-
troduced terrorism into international affairs, provoked three
wars between the Arab states and Israel, as well as a form of
civil war between Palestinians of the occupied territories and
Israeli authorities and colonists, and produced civil war, national disintegration, and foreign occupation in Lebanon. It
made the United States, as Israel's sponsor, into an object of
popular anger throughout the region.

   But the United States was also the object of hatred combined with fascination as avatar of a culturally and economi-
cally aggressive modern West whose challenge to Islamic

society is the fundamental cause of the crisis which existed   *119*
there before there was an Israel. This is a crisis having to do
with the capacity of a civilization to respond to historical
change. Islam, Judaism, and Christianity are the dominant
religions of mankind today because they are intellectually
alive in ways Hinduism and Buddhism are not. All are com-
bative, confident, historically intolerant systems of values
and ways of life. But for Islam, religious conviction no longer
translates into cultural or political confidence.

The uneasiness within Islamic society about the Islamic
way of life in the twentieth century derives from two related
problems. The first is Islam's failure to formulate a modern
conception of politics and government capable of dealing
with a non-Islamic world much more powerful in material
means, organization, and science. The second problem is the
practical consequence of that discrepancy of power, the colonial legacy: that resentment and sense of powerlessness en-
gendered within Islam by its domination by the West since
the late eighteenth and early nineteenth centuries—since
Britain's conquest of Moghul India and assertion of effective
domination over Persia and Egypt, France's conquest of
North Africa, and the defeat and dismemberment of the Ottoman Empire. Added to that have been Israel's repeated military humiliations of the Arabs since the 1948 war, and the
1991 defeat of Iraq, the strongest of the Arab states, by a
coalition of the United States and the European powers, supported by the Soviet Union, with allies even inside the Arab
world itself. The politico-psychological impact of that crisis
was intensified by the fact that the Arab states themselves
were divided by this conflict, which was produced by one
Arab state's act of aggression against another. Saudi Arabia,
Egypt, Syria, Morocco, and the Gulf states supported the

THE WRATH OF NATIONS

120 UN intervention. It was further evidence of Arab division
and powerlessness.

Writing before the Second World War, Arnold Toynbee
observed that the Moslems, who some thirteen centuries before had committed themselves to the "proud but unproven
belief" that God had given them, in their religion, guarantee
of a unique destiny in this world as well as in the next, "and,
in the strength of it, performed . . . mighty deeds in their
earlier history, have had time enough to fall on evil days; and
the feebleness of their reaction to their latter-day tribula-
tions indicates that Determinism is just as apt to sap *moral* in
adversity as it is to stimulate it so long as the challenges encountered are within the range of an effective response." Of
the plight of "the disillusioned predestinarian" who has discovered that God is perhaps not, after all, on his side, Toynbee quoted (FitzGerald's) "Rubáiyát" itself:

> *But helpless Pieces in the Game [God] plays*
> *Upon this Chequer-board of Nights and Days;*
> *   Hither and thither moves, and checks, and slays,*
> *And one by one back in the Closet lays.*

A sense of victimization and impotence lies behind the
phenomenon of revolutionary Islamic integrism or fundamentalism, which looks for a remedy for Islam's powerlessness in religious orthodoxy and the theocratic state. Islamic
fundamentalism responds to a crisis of Islamic political and
historical consciousness begun even before the Ottoman collapse at the beginning of this century, which the military and
political confrontations of recent years with Israel and the
other western powers have merely intensified.

The sixth-century origins of Islam lie in a reaction in
Arabia against foreign interference, that of Abyssinia, Persia,
and Byzantium, during the period prior to Mohammed's
birth in 570. It was a patriotic as well as a religious movement, advocating, as an Edwardian scholar says, "Arabia for
the Arabians." Mohammed unified Arabia, and by the time of
his death in 632 foreign power in Arabia had been broken.
The first war waged by the Caliphs was against the Persians—to subdue Iraq, which then belonged to Persia. The
pertinence of this to what has happened again in recent years
need not be labored.

Islam's religious determinism was a great source of
power when things were going well, as determinism was later
for predestinarian Calvinists and Marxists, "satisf[ying] the
same hunger for an assurance that the forces of the Universe
are on the side of the Elect," as R. H. Tawney has remarked.
Just as Calvinism allowed the bourgeoisie of the sixteenth
century, and Marxism the proletariat of the nineteenth and
twentieth centuries (and the middle-class intellectuals who
appointed themselves the proletariat's leaders), "to feel that
they were a Chosen People, . . . [making] them conscious of
their great destiny in the Providential plan and resolute to
realize it," Islam's conviction of predetermined victory inspired a superb confidence during Islam's early period of
hardly stoppable expansion. The Arabs swept out from the
Arabian peninsula to Gibraltar, Spain, and France in one direction and nearly to China in the other. But once they were
stopped, and the European powers turned a new kind of organizational and technological power against them, to which
they had no adequate response, the effect of their predestinarianism was reversed and a corrosive doubt created, which
plays upon them today: that defeat was all along inevitable.

•

The Arabs' was a politically sophisticated empire despite
the migration of the "universal empire's" power center from
Damascus to Baghdad, and eventually to Ottoman Istanbul.
Islamic civilization possessed a rich literature and philosophy, and an advanced theoretical science. It possessed the
high technology of the period, with more advanced military
organization than medieval Europe. It won the Crusades and
the battles of Islam's expansion in Spain, France, and Eastern
Europe. Poitiers, Lepanto, Vienna—the great turning
points—were, for the Christians overall, damned near-run
things. Had the Venetians and Spaniards failed at Lepanto,
the French at Poitiers, or the Austrians and Poles at Vienna
in 1683, the western readers of this book might well be
Moslems. Gibbon has a famous passage considering the possibility of Koranic instruction in the schools of Oxford, had
Charles Martel lost.

However, the real reason for the West's successful defense, and subsequent victory over Islam, was not western
military capacity. It was the ability of Europe in the Renaissance, and subsequently the Enlightenment, to reexamine
the fundamentals of its own religion and civilization in the
light of the thought of pagan antiquity and a philosophical
and scientific rationalism. With respect to material power,
Europeans passed from an artisanal technology and theocen-
tric science to empirical science and industrial technology
and manufacture. Why this transition should have occurred
in Europe and not in the Islamic world no doubt has to do in
part with mere hazards of history and of intellectual development in different societies. It must also connect with the social and cultural roots of the two civilizations. The Jewish
and Christian Bible begins with God's commission to Adam,

in Genesis, to rule over the earth and its creatures; and western civilization has since been distinguished by an ex-
ploratory and exploitative approach to the animal kingdom
and the material universe. The western belief that the world
and history itself are to be mastered to man's advantage has
its origin here. Hence the great fourteenth- and fifteenth-
century Portuguese, Spanish, and English voyages of exploration, and the intellectual adventurousness which even in
the Middle Ages produced secular explanations of astronom-
ical and physical forces and ideas of flying machines and a
natural energy. Such ideas obviously also existed among the
antique Greeks. Icarus belongs to a separate and convergent
western tradition of defiance of limit, described by reference
to still another Greek figure, Prometheus. The Greeks'
stealing of fire has brought us to the nuclear explosion. The
West's is, one concedes, an ambiguous legacy.

The identification of religion with civilization in Islamic
society blocks a solution to its contemporary problems.
Christianity from the beginning distinguished between religion and the political, secular order. There were "things that
are Caesar's"—legitimately due to Caesar, ruler of an autonomous political and social order. Because of this distinction, it was possible for Europe to develop secular knowledge,
a secular culture, and, eventually, even largely to cast off the
influence of religion. (How complete, or lasting, this aban-
donment of religion will prove to be is another question.
There is, as a Viennese medical theoretician and practitioner
greatly influencing this development has said, a return of the
repressed.)
    Islam is a priestless religion, unhierarchical, largely with-
out a modern speculative theology. The absence of this has

124   inhibited intellectual and scientific reflection, which might
have introduced doubt about the religious interpretation of
natural phenomena, as happened in the West, but which
would also have made possible a more vigorous response to
the intellectual challenge of the West. The remarkable Arab
philosophical flowering of the early Middle Ages, notable
above all for Avicenna and the Spaniard Averroës, faded away
toward the end of the twelfth century in a revival of religious
orthodoxy and intolerance associated with the rise in influence of the recently converted Turkish peoples from Central
Asia. The thinkers associated with classical Greek influences
were silenced. (Averroës' subsequent influence was most
marked on the Jewish scholars of Languedoc and Provence,
who had been expelled from Spain, and on the Christians
Albertus Magnus, Thomas Aquinas, Duns Scotus, and Roger
Bacon. Averroism, reinterpreted, eventually became, in the
schools of northern Italy, the philosophy of Christian theological skepticism and the new scientific thought.)

There is irony in the fact that Arab scholars preserved
Greek philosophy from the ninth to twelfth centuries and
transmitted it to medieval Europe, making it possible for
Aquinas to develop a rationalist theological and philosophical system that reconciled pagan Greek thought with Christian thought, the very thing Islam failed to accomplish.
Aquinas held that the two sources of knowledge are human
reason, which Aristotle exemplified, and divine revelation,
and while the latter must be privileged, the former is totally
valid in itself. This provided the secular intelligence with autonomous authority and made possible a philosophical response to the developing modern world for which there was
no equivalent in Islam.

There, philosophy, like literature, remained, and remains, bound to the Koran. There has been an Islamic political philosophy and even a political "science," in that the nature of rule, and the problems of authority and administration, have been the subjects of reflection since classical Islamic times, and Greek political philosophy has been incorporated into the Arabic literature on governing. But in the Islamic world, the eminent American Islamist Bernard Lewis says, "[t]he principal function of government is to enable the individual Muslim to lead a good Muslim life. This is, in the last analysis, the purpose of the state, for which alone it is established by God, and for which alone statesmen are given authority over others. The worth of the state, and the good and evil deeds of statesmen, are measured by the extent to which this purpose is accomplished."

This has decisively inhibited the development of suitable concepts for a modern politics, even though the actual practices of the modern western nation, often the worst practices, have readily been adapted by the heads of modern Middle Eastern states. It also is significant that the shah of Iran, Saddam Hussein of Iraq, several of the modern leaders of Egypt, and Atatürk in Turkey all tried to associate their rule with pre-Moslem history: with the ancient Persian monarchs, Mesopotamia, pharaonic Egypt, and so on. When observant Moslems try to rule without westernized systems and ideas they are left with the unsolved problems of the young Iranian intellectuals around the Ayatollah Ruhollah Khomeini in the 1970s: how to define an "Islamic economics," an "Islamic finance," an Islamic way to run industry.

No doubt it is significant too that among Islam's early followers were nomads with a predominantly oral and literary culture. This has been a source of immense confusion in

126   the wars of rhetorical abuse conducted in the twentieth century between Palestinians and the Arab capitals on the one
hand, and the western governments on the other. Lewis ob-
serves that when Iraq and Iran were at war in the Gulf in the
1980s, propaganda on both sides made "frequent allusions to
events of the seventh and eighth centuries. There can be little doubt that these references are recognized by the vast majority of people in both countries and indeed elsewhere in
the Muslim world, and that the force of the allusions is well
understood."*

The scientific and technological failure of Islamic civilization has perhaps reflected the largely fixed technological
demands of Arab empire, nomadic in origins; there may have
been a lack of development because, except in the military
sphere, there was no great demand for it. Yet early-medieval
Arabia's science and mathematics were more advanced than
Europe's. The failure occurred between the late Middle Ages
and the seventeenth century. Whatever the explanation, and
there is no simple explanation for it, the West decisively sur-
passed Islamic society in its capacity for scientific development and social organization and administration, creating a

---

*The capacity for historical reference of the American political class, not
to speak of the American public, risks exhaustion once Munich, Hitler,
Holocaust, Cuban missile crisis, and Vietnam are cited. Czeslaw Milosz's
remarks in his 1980 Nobel Prize lecture are worth notice in this respect:
"Our planet, which grows smaller every year with its fantastic prolifera-
tion of mass media, is witnessing a process that defies definition, characterized by a refusal to remember. . . . In the mind of modern illiterates . . .
who know to read and write and even teach in schools and universities,
history is present but blurred, in a state of strange confusion. . . . [E]vents
of the last decades, of such primary importance that knowledge or ignorance of them will be decisive for the future of mankind, move away, grow
pale, lose all consistency, as if Friedrich Nietzsche's prediction of European nihilism found a literal fulfillment. . . ."

modern industrial technology, modern forms of government **127** and of international society, and the modern speculative and analytical intellectual culture.

Efforts to deal with this problem have been made by Islamic intellectuals and scholars in Southern and Central Asia as well as the Middle East since the nineteenth century and before. An "Anglo-Oriental" college was founded in Aligarh in India in 1875, modeled on a Cambridge college but teaching in Urdu. Similar undertakings were sponsored by Tatar merchants in the Volga Valley and other Moslem regions of the Russian Empire. Modernizers were active at Al-Azhar University in Cairo in the late nineteenth and early twentieth centuries, and in Algeria, where many educated Algerians were simply abandoning Islam for French civilization. But these efforts ran into the problem modernizers have faced everywhere in the non-western world (not just in Islamic society). If one excludes the unrealizable alternative of reactionary revival—what the Islamic fundamentalists want to accomplish today, although they will fail—and on the other hand rejects total conversion to western ideas and standards, what remains is the necessity to make a synthesis of civilizations.

This is a tremendously ambitious undertaking, which, even if it succeeds, or comes close to doing so, is likely still to lack authenticity and practicality as a program for the ordinary people in what remains an integrally religious society. There are hundreds of thousands of cultivated Moslems who have made creative individual syntheses of Islamic and western influences and education. (There are many others for whom the effort has been a destructive experience.) But what works for the individual has thus far been impossible as a coherent program for a society. The westernization or "synthe-

128   sis" which actually threatens to engulf the masses in the Islamic world, as in much of the non-western world, is junk westernization: their submersion by a tide of western mass commercial culture, usually American, cut free from the civilization that manufactured it and (presumably) knows how to handle it.

The "national" struggle of the Islamic countries, the "Arab nationalist" movements that have come and gone, the idea of the "Arab nation" itself, all have been expressions of a crisis which has very little to do with the modern nation but is that of a religion and its relationship with the modern secular and scientific civilization of the West. The grievances (and grief) of modern Islam, its paranoia and defiance, follow from that.

Islamic fundamentalism is a form of "national" resistance, an assertion of political autonomy and independence vis-à-vis the western powers, and an attempt to reclaim a jeopardized cultural independence and wholeness, in which statehood or nationhood is merely means to an end. Iran, where the fundamentalist movement first came to power, has more than any other Middle or Near Eastern country been the victim of western domination. As early as the seventeenth century it came under the indirect influence of Britain, which was determined to control the land routes of communication to India. The United States took over Britain's role in the 1950s, restoring the young shah to power against a genuinely nationalist movement which wanted Persia/Iran's oil as well as its government under Iranian control. Three centuries of foreign interference had by the 1960s produced a condition of something like political paranoia among Iranians, who were convinced that they had lost all control over their own destinies. Even Muhammad Reza Shah's megalomaniacal plans for Iran, that it become the world's "fifth superpower" (after the U.S., the U.S.S.R., Japan, and united Europe), cynically encouraged by Richard Nixon and Henry Kissinger, were perceived by other Iranians as a fantasy alien to Iran's interests and values. The shah increasingly tried to associate his regime symbolically with the pre-Islamic dynasties of Persia, the more so as economic development and the premium placed on material values in his Iran undermined Islamic norms of piety and virtue. The fundamentalist reaction was a repudiation of these efforts quite as much as it was a revolt against the power the United States had come to possess in Iran's government and economy. It was an act of cultural desperation, born of despair. The promise it offered was that of a restored Islamic golden age. But this is unachievable.

Throughout the Islamic world, the fundamentalist movement is a product of the failure of secular nationalism. The dream of the Arab nation has ended in the squalid Ba'athist dictatorships in power in Syria and Iraq. Revolutionary "Arab socialism" bestowed military dictatorships on Egypt and Algeria, conducting disastrously irrelevant programs of heavy industrial development. The regimes which have survived in the postwar half century are the conservative monarchies in Saudi Arabia, Jordan, and Morocco. In each case the monarch's legitimacy has been linked to his religious role as descendant of the Prophet or protector of the Holy Places. But reasonable doubt exists about the capacity of these dynasties to survive after the present monarchs are gone.

As the golden age cannot be reclaimed, and the cultural crisis deepens under the assault of westernized consumerism and popular communications, with existing governments in-

130   capable of a positive response to the western challenge, it is
necessary to assume that the Middle Eastern crisis will grow
worse. The fundamentalist movement is virtually the only
available recourse or consolation, at least for the masses of
Islamic society. Intellectuals have the possibility of a personal synthesis of influences, an individual accommodation
and transcendence, and even the choice of exile; but that
does no good for Islamic society as a whole.

It consequently is difficult to see anything other than
continuing internal conflict in the Islamic world, and, for a
time, the steady progress of fundamentalism as a means to
beat off the West's threat to the inherited values of Islam.
This effort will not succeed, but it is perhaps unimportant
that it will not succeed. Islam will make its way through the
cultural crisis produced by this failure to develop secular
thought and political theory, a modern science, a theology
capable of serious dialogue with the post-Enlightenment intellectual society of the West. The violence and sporadic terrorism which accompany the fundamentalist movement will
be of consequence chiefly for the Islamic countries.

It is the essential characteristic of fundamentalism that
it is defensive, isolationist, preoccupied with protecting Islam against the West. It is not expansionist: the fundamentalists would not dream of attempting to overrun western
societies even if that were possible. They are in flight from
the West. Why would they want to incorporate still more of
the West and its civilization within their own religious frontiers? They wish to convert Moslems living in the West to
their values in order to have their sympathy and support, or
to convince them to return to piety and security in the Islamic countries. The fundamentalists are like Zionists in this

respect. They do not imagine converting other peoples. They want to rally and radicalize their own, to defend and reinvigorate their own society. But they offer no fundamental solution to Islam's problem. Their past, their Islamic golden age, is as irreclaimable as the integral Christianity of the western Middle Ages is to those who live in modern America or Europe.

The experience of Islam, over the last three centuries, has been of intellectual and moral subjection to the West. However, its defeats have never been accepted as final and, having not been so accepted, cannot be considered conclusive, even by those in the West who remain in the dominating position. The integrist or fundamentalist movement is one more refusal of defeat, a characteristic one, if a doomed one. The secular, militarized, quasi-socialist Arab or pan-Arab "nationalist" movements that still govern in Baghdad, Damascus, and Algiers as the end of the twentieth century approaches are also forms of resistance, if no more successful. The dictatorships, together with the fundamentalist movement, with its frantic, even hysterical, resistance to western influences and to all those in Islamic society whom its members believe compromised by the West, attest to the intellectual defeat—admittedly provisional—of one people and one religion by another civilization, the West, with which the first has always been intimately connected and morally rival.

6 *Asian and African Nationalism*

One speaks uneasily of nations, or even of empires in Asia, other than the European empires created there, because it is not clear that what in the past existed there were nations or empires in any sense useful to contemporary political discussion. China was a civilization ruled by a centralized bureaucracy. It may from our anachronistic viewpoint be considered either an empire or nation; but surely the Chinese were not conscious of being other than the inevitable order of things?

It seems better to say that in Asia there were and are civilizations, agrarian, cultural, moral in quality, each with a self-sufficient political existence, but not in the past a national existence; and certainly they were innocent of nationalism. They were aware of themselves as specific political entities only on those distant frontiers where other civilizations were encountered—or, more often, "barbarians," inferior in culture and political strength. These were either to be conquered, forced into submission and tribute, or assimilated. China and India both experienced "barbarian" conquest by nomads from Central Asia, the Manchus and

Moghuls. Neither yielded its own identity or cultural autonomy, but "civilized" and thereby conquered the invaders,
making the Manchus into Chinese and the Moghuls Indians—higher forms of mankind, as all eventually were willing
to believe. The conquerors gladly abandoned their previous
condition as rude nomads of the steppes.

The existence and preeminence of these empires was
thought by their subjects to be the natural order itself, to
which no serious alternative existed. What did exist outside
this civilization might merit curiosity, but surely no great
concern. It was a novelty in China and Japan (a Chinese cultural tributary, like Korea) that evil-smelling foreigners
should land on their shores in the Christian sixteenth century to propose trade for their sophisticated goods, their
spices and materials, but this was not considered a phenomenon worth serious attention until much later—which proved,
for the Chinese, too late.

The Japanese were more prudent than the Chinese (or
the Indian princes). Observing that the Christian Europeans
had by the sixteenth century already installed themselves in
the Philippines, an unsophisticated and uncentralized Malay
society, the Japanese authorities decided to isolate and eventually to exclude Europeans from their country, and they
persecuted or killed the Christian converts these had made
among the Japanese. The Chinese were more confident of
themselves, or arrogant, and were to pay the price for this in
the nineteenth and twentieth centuries.

In the nineteenth century the European powers completed what Portugal and Spain had begun in the fifteenth
century. They had overrun every part of Africa and Asia they
could reach. Imperialism awakened sub-Saharan Africa, dis-

134   turbed before only by the rise and fall of circumscribed kingdoms that left art behind them, but no words. It broke the
circularities of the great Asian civilizations, as it had already
done to those of the Aztecs and Maya in the Americas, destroying the latter, forcing the former to defend themselves
by rethinking themselves—which they did, so that after
much grief and struggle they made themselves into political
nations on the European model. Before, China, India, and
Persia had simply been imperial civilizations. In the twentieth century they became nations. Asian nationalism thus is a
modern phenomenon, like European nationalism. What existed before the twentieth century in Asia was a resistance to
colonialism, and, fundamentally, to European intrusion, and
this was cultural rather than political in quality.

West European imperialism was not national aggrandizement as such, since the European powers did not intend
to annex overseas territories in order to make them part of
themselves (as, say, Rome had done; France's making Algeria
a *département* of France was an exception to this, and a serious mistake, as the war of 1954–1962 later demonstrated).
They wanted access to trade and resources, expanded military power, the spread of Christian religion, prestige, the radiation of their own civilizations.

This was not the case for the other European empire, often ignored in discussions of nationalism, that of Russia. Russia's was a nationalism-driven imperialism which annexed to
Russia a Central Asia whose largely nomadic peoples had five
hundred years earlier themselves commanded "the largest
contiguous land empire that has so far existed." The Mongols'
empire in the thirteenth and fourteenth centuries "[a]t its
greatest extent stretched from Korea to Hungary, including,

except for India and the south-east of the continent, most of
Asia, as well as a good deal of eastern Europe . . . [and] was
merely one, albeit by far the most extensive, of a series of
great steppe empires" (to quote a contemporary historian of
the Mongols, David Morgan of the University of London).

This empire's fall, and western Mongolia's subsequent
conquest by Russia, was the result of its inability to evolve; its
unsophisticated methods of organization and administration
failed to meet the demands of ruling so extensive a conquest.
Its cosmology was primitive; its religion, a shamanism including blood sacrifices, was eventually supplanted in the
east by a Buddhist Lamaism imported from Tibet, part of the
process by which China absorbed eastern Mongolia, while
western Mongolia became Moslem and eventually, after a
long period of isolation and obscurity, was taken into Russian
possession or indirect rule in the eighteenth and nineteenth
centuries.

There are today more Mongolians inside China's frontiers than in Mongolia itself, while Mongolia proper became
a People's Republic under Bolshevik domination in the
1920s, although still largely run by Mongolians. Nothing of
what happened to Mongolia prior to the claim to independence that was made when the Soviet system collapsed can
properly be described in the languages of nations and nationalism. Seven decades under centralized Soviet rule, subject to
Soviet policies of Russification, urbanization, the settlement
of nomads and industrialization, with an international role to
play at the United Nations, may have produced a degree of
national consciousness which did not exist before. It is notable that Genghis Khan is a figure rehabilitated in the Mon-
golian Republic since it gained its independence from the
U.S.S.R.

•

The vital role of western ideas in the Asian transition from self-sufficient dynastic political existence to modern nationhood is often underestimated today, when it is no longer fashionable to talk about civilizations in terms of superiority or inferiority. China, Japan, and India, like Egypt and Persia, have never been the inferiors of the West in sophistication or subtlety of thought and discourse, or in artistic power. But in technique, science, and organizational and administrative capacity they were in the eighteenth and nineteenth centuries, like Moslem societies, hopelessly outclassed by the West. Since then, only Japan has fully recovered from this inferiority. In the struggle between these civilizations the assimilative attraction, the impulse to conversion, has been towards the invading West, at the same time that the contradictory urge to expel foreign influences has mounted. This was the essential drama of modern Asia until the 1980s, when, in the realm of political power at least, the expulsion was finally achieved.*

The reactions against colonialism which gathered force in Asia during the nineteenth and early twentieth centuries, reaching their successful climax after World War II, can be called "nationalist" only in a very approximate way. There is slight resemblance between them and Europe's nineteenth-century nationalisms. In Asia there were suppressed peo-

*With the closing of contested U.S. military bases in the Philippines, a former Pacific colony of the United States, and the scheduled British withdrawal from Hong Kong in 1997, the western Pacific empires come to their end. American forces remain in South Korea and Japan, but the movement of opinion in Asia has shifted and this residual American military presence in the region tends now to be seen as a desirable factor for stability in the not entirely predictable relations among China, Japan, Russia, and their neighboring states.

ples—tribal peoples, aboriginals, religious minorities—but their oppressors were other Asians with whom they had co-existed throughout remembered time. These were not "foreign," so the cultural barrier between oppressed and oppressor ordinarily was not great. The principal conquered peoples were the Hindu Indians, who from the sixteenth century forward were ruled by Moslem Moghuls (Turkish and Afghan invaders), and the Chinese, who from 1644 to 1912 were under the rule of the Manchus, pastoral nomads from Manchuria. In both cases the conquered were more sophisticated than the conquerors, and in essential respects absorbed them into their own civilizations.

This was not the case when the European imperialists came. In the beginning, the Europeans had no significant material or military advantage over the Asians. Their military power was slight by comparison with that which the Chinese emperor or Japanese shoguns might have deployed against their expeditions. India was conquered by the British with a handful of men and an astute manipulation of powerful Indian princes, one against another. Japan isolated itself. The Chinese imperial authorities allowed trading settlements, so that eventually coastal and commercial China was parceled out to several European powers, the United States (in the guise of imposing a fair division on the others, an "Open Door" to China), and finally (and fatefully) Japan, once Japan set out to give itself its own western-style empire. What now is Indonesia was, when the Europeans came, a set of distinct Moslem Malay sultanates and Hindu kingdoms, major spice exporters, the former having accepted the suzerainty of the Chinese emperor. The region was at the center of the rival expansions of Hindu, Moslem, and Christian civilizations. Of the European contenders, the Nether-

138   lands eventually dominated, and remained the principal colonizer until Japan, in 1941, suddenly and dramatically drove
the Dutch out of the East Indies.

Before the nineteenth century, had any of the Asians resisted European invasion with anything resembling the fe-
rocity and popular mobilization of Vietnam's resistance to
France and the United States in the twentieth century, or
that of the Indonesians against the Dutch, European power
would never have been installed in Asia. Most Asian rulers
remained complacently confident of their superiority over
the piratical intruders from incomprehensibly (and uninter-
estingly) remote places. Such confidence was part of the very
structure and assumption of Chinese civilization. The notion
of an equally sophisticated and more powerful Other, arriv-
ing from an unknown region of the world, was, to the Chinese, an untenable, even unimaginable, hypothesis.

The Indian historian K. M. Panikkar writes of his own
country that as late as 1750 "[i]t would have required super-
natural vision for an observer . . . to foretell that in the
course of fifty years a European nation would have conquered a third of India and would be preparing to contest
with the Marathas for a position of paramountcy over the
rest." The robber state created by Clive for the East India
Company was turned into a well-organized civil and military
administration dominating India until the uprising of
1857–1858, known in British history as the Indian (or Sepoy)
Mutiny, and to Indians today as the Great Rebellion. After
that, the British crown assumed power over India, the British
government administering the country directly for nearly a
century, until 1950.

The uprising had been the last effort of the old ruling

groups to drive out the British, but it acquired its power from **139**
the popular distress caused by the threat the British presence
posed to the religious and social values of both Hindus and
Moslems. This was to characterize Asian resistance to the
West to the present day. The rebellion was touched off by a
rumor in both communities that the cartridge grease in
which Indian army ammunition was packed was ritually un-
clean to both Hindus and Moslems, but the scale of the popular reaction was caused not simply by abuse of Asian
religious conventions but by reform itself, progressive and
enlightened in British eyes. A British historian wrote at the
end of the century that in Bengal, where the rebellion began,
"the Brahmins were offended at the prohibition of suttee
[the forced immolation of widows] and female infanticide,
the execution of Brahmins for capital offenses, the remar-
riage of widows, the spread of [Christian] missionary efforts
and the extension of Western education."

The rebellion can scarcely be called a nationalist uprising in the modern sense, nor were the revolts of the period
elsewhere, ferocious ones in Java early in the nineteenth century and in Bali in 1906 and 1908. These were, again, primarily cultural in character rather than political, motivated by
popular distress at the Europeans' challenge to the cultural
underpinnings of Asian societies.

This resistance often took a religiously syncretist character, as in the Taiping (great peace) upheaval in China in
1850–1864, in which millions were killed. The Taiping
movement was launched by a semi-literate village school-
master who had been the pupil of an American Protestant
missionary. He announced that he was the younger brother
of Christ, denounced Buddhism, Taoism, and Confucianism
as idolatry, preached against concubinage, and called for

140   land reform and an end to slavery, opium use, arranged marriage and foot-binding for women. He demanded social equality and the communal reorganization of society—all to huge popular effect. His was a form of primitive communist doctrine with marked resemblances to twentieth-century Maoism. In both cases a western-motivated social criticism of Chinese injustices was assimilated into a movement with traditional Chinese characteristics, and the result was a popular mobilization for what was simultaneously an antiforeign reaction and a social protest. The external criticism of Chinese society was, so to speak, internalized, and for that reason acquired a power it would not otherwise have possessed.

Comparable syncretist religio-political phenomena involving the simultaneous rejection of the West and attempted annexation of its values (or powers) have existed in colonial Africa since the late nineteenth century. They are what Vittorio Lanternari has called "religions of the oppressed." In Vietnam, the Cao Dai remains the best known of contemporary Asian syncretisms, incorporating Victor Hugo and figures from the French Enlightenment into its pantheon, where Christ and the Buddha also figure. Taiwan since the 1920s has had its syncretist version of the Jehovah's Witnesses sect, founded by a Chinese known as Watchman Ni, who rejected the forms of Christian worship put forward by conventional Anglo-American missionaries. (The Jehovah's Witnesses or Watchtower church was also the source of one of the syncretist sects of the ex–Belgian Congo, in Africa.) There are neo-Buddhist and quasi-Christian sects in Japan and Korea today (as well as among the socially or emotionally marginalized in the United States) possessing similar characteristics.

In Africa, the most pathetic case is that of the suicide of 141
the Xhosa people in 1857 when, after their military defeat in
a savage war with the British, they listened to the prophetic
message of a fifteen-year-old girl who claimed that she was
transmitting a message from the afterworld: that the Xhosa
should kill all their cattle, cease to cultivate their fields, and
scatter their food stores. After that—as J. M. Coetzee has re-
counted the affair, "[a] day of reckoning would follow: a new
sun would rise, the British would be swallowed into the sea,
there would be a grand resurrection of the ancestors; then
would follow an earthquake, after which new herds of cattle,
immortal, would emerge from under the earth, and new corn
stand in the fields." The date when this was to occur was February 18, 1857, and when it did not, those who had believed
turned in murderous rage upon the unbelievers who were
held to be responsible. Tens of thousands died, and "the integrity of Xhosa culture was shattered." (One must ask if
comparable expectations today may not have been attached
to the achievement of a new South Africa by some supporters
of the predominantly Xhosa African National Congress.)

Other African nativist cults have included the Kitawala
and Kimbangu, the "Antonians," and the Epikilipikili prophetic sect in the Congo; and as the current breakdown of
African economic and social structures goes on, there no
doubt will be more.

Islamic fundamentalism is also a religion of the oppressed, of the kind that promises a re-created golden age.
The Indian rebellion and the so-called Boxer Uprising in
China conformed to this same model of reaction to western
intrusion. In India in the 1850s, the mutinous sepoys proclaimed (vainly) a revival of the Moghul Empire when, after

142   two years of fighting, they finally reached Delhi. In China, the Boxers' slogan was "Cherish the Dynasty—Exterminate the Foreigner." The Boxers (an English-language name literally translated from the Chinese "fist of righteous harmony") rejected the westernizing reforms begun in Peking in 1898, enjoying the implied patronage of the young emperor Kuang-hsü. The reformers proposed to replace the ancient examination system for the public administration with one based on western knowledge. A government department was to be created for the translation and dissemination of western works. Officials were to be compelled to study foreign languages and travel abroad. It was contemplated that the queue or pigtail would be abolished (originally imposed on the Chinese by the Manchus as a sign of subjugation, but by now a "national" symbol).

The Manchu court, dominated by the dowager empress, was against such changes and covertly encouraged the Boxer movement, which began with the murder of a western missionary and proposed to exterminate Christian missionaries and "secondary barbarians"—their Chinese converts—seen as embodying the essential western challenge to old Chinese society. The Boxers took over northern China and occupied Peking with the connivance of the court authorities, but eventually were put down by military intervention by the western powers and Japan, which occupied Peking in 1900.

These movements were produced by the popular cultural distress produced by the invasion of foreign civilizations not only materially more powerful than their Asian victims but also possessing a moral certainty about their right to rule over Asians. The Europeans were confident that they were the Asians' superiors not only in science, invention, and commerce but, as the English scholar G. F. Hudson

says, in "moral science. . . . The Englishman especially, who 143
was the chief representative of Europe in relations with
China during the nineteenth century, had ascended by 1850
[in his own estimation] to a moral elevation which would
have been incredible to his great-grandfather."

The nineteenth-century British believed they were, in
the Platonic sense, guardians, bringing order, justice, and
enlightenment. Philip Woodruff, a historian of the British in
India, writes, "The similarities to Plato's state were uncon-
scious but they were based on a deep admiration for Plato . . .
throughout the English upper classes, and it was in Plato that
the contradiction lay. Plato's state was one which Englishmen would never have tolerated for themselves. . . . Yet just
such a rule they did themselves impose on India."

For Victorian and Edwardian Englishmen the contradiction was not apparent. It was the struggle to rescue British
principle from British practice that eventually made India
into a democracy in 1950, even if that had never been the intention.* Panikkar writes of the Brahmo Samaj movement
among Hindu intellectuals in the second decade of the nineteenth century, which wanted "westernization, to purge Hinduism of the customs and superstitions with which it was
overlaid, to raise the status of women, to bridge the yawning

---

*While India today remains a fragile democracy, under intense pressure
from the communal tensions within Indian society, it is the sole case, thus
far, of a colonized Asian civilization becoming a democracy and remain-
ing one. The case is admittedly paradoxical in that Jawaharlal Nehru, independent India's first prime minister, father of secular and democratic
India, and the very model of the secularized and westernized Hindu, in
fact proves to have established a political dynasty. Thirty years after his
death, the Italian widow of his grandson Sanjay Gandhi is the most powerful individual influence on the ruling Congress party as it awaits the expected succession to power of still another of Nehru's descendants, his
great-granddaughter.

144 gulf between popular and higher Hinduism, to fight relent-
lessly against caste, social taboo, polygamy. . . . To the educated Hindu, who felt unsettled in mind by the attack of the
missionaries, . . . [it] provided the way out." It was not the
way out. The assumption of European moral superiority and
guardianship was finally undermined only in the twentieth
century, and with it the belief that Europeans—above all,
Englishmen—possessed the natural right to rule "backward"
peoples, "natives." Those words themselves went out of the
vocabulary.

Europe's prestige was ruined by the First World War, a
suicidal European civil war of an intensity and scale never
before seen, into which the European powers drafted Indian
regiments, Senegalese and Moroccan infantry and cavalry,
and Indochinese and Chinese auxiliaries, while implicat-
ing—to its fatal misfortune—Ottoman Turkey. The notion
of the moral superiority of the West was finished in Asia after
that, surviving only with respect to the United States, which
between the wars and for a brief period after World War II
continued to enjoy the reputation of a liberating power, and
itself continued, until its defeat in Vietnam, to believe that it
was capable of conveying political enlightenment to backward peoples.

One might think that China, an ancient and supremely
self-sufficient society, would have been capable of a "national" resistance to the West—dealing with the Europeans
on self-confident terms, adapting western methods and ideas
to its own purposes, making a valid cultural synthesis. This
was accomplished by Japan in the nineteenth and twentieth
centuries (if at great political and social cost, including that of
a brutal and failed imperialism, ended by world war). China's

formidable classical age was contemporary with that of Greece. From the fifth to fifteenth centuries it was the most advanced civilization on earth in applying material knowledge to human needs, Europe's clear superior in science and technology. But China did not experience a Newtonian revolution; its science did not become a modern science, and by the eighteenth century it had fallen decisively behind the European colonial nations in economic and technological power.

The argument is made (following Karl Wittfogel) that the successful centralization of power in China had produced a political system which was rigid and absolutist (and, according to Wittfogel, pretotalitarian) because government's authority rested on its construction and maintenance of the immense irrigation systems upon which the agricultural economy depended. This enterprise required elaborate and disciplined bureaucratic administration. The social ideal in such a society was therefore the administrator, selected through meritocratic examination, hence the scholar-administrator, and beyond that the scholar-gentleman. Merchants and soldiers had low prestige. The entrepreneurial and innovative merchant middle classes which modernized the West thus never became a decisive force in China.*

*A contemporary western counterpart, on a minor scale, is England, where the dominant social ideal remains aristocratic and agricultural, that of the gentleman landowner. Generations of newly successful merchants and entrepreneurs have been grateful to have their sons co-opted to an aristocratic ethos which disparages trade. Britain's great capitalists and engineers have nearly all come from nonestablished social groups and dissenting religious communities, and from Scotland, Northern Ireland, and the colonies. John Major, whose father was a circus performer, is the latest British leader from such a background, and he made the electoral promise to create a classless society, but his Conservative predecessor, a grocer's daughter, accepted ennoblement herself when she left office, and arranged a hereditary title for her son, despite his innocence of any credentials of public service. Her Labour predecessor, Harold Wilson, a university

•

The vulnerability of the Chinese Empire to the aggressive dynastic nation-states that emerged in Europe was evident in the fact that Renaissance Europe knew a good deal about China, and China had a marked influence on taste and sensibility in Europe, while the Chinese knew next to nothing about Europe, and did not wish to know. The Chinese belief in themselves as the center of civilization, with no need of outside contact, persisted through the years of Ming decline in the sixteenth and seventeenth centuries. Such complacence was not unfounded. Those Europeans who knew China at the period (some as observant prisoners of the Chinese) found it a more sophisticated society than contemporary Europe, and more advanced in practical ways.

Juan Gonsalez de Mendoza, a Spanish priest involved in an ultimately unsuccessful sixteenth-century attempt to establish a Christian mission in the country, wrote, in a work whose English translation was published in 1588, that China's government seemed "worthily accounted one of the best . . . in all the world," with justice impartially administered by magistrates under objective supervision, the death penalty rare, and death sentences always reviewed by a higher court. He wrote that everywhere, even in the mountains, highways were paved, pitched to drain, and carefully maintained. Cities seemed magnificent, the homes of officials "superbious and admirable, and wrought by marvellous art, and are as big as a great village by reason that they have within them great gardens, water ponds and woods com-

---

teacher also of modest origins, ended his term at Downing Street with an extraordinary distribution of honors and ennoblements to political cronies, allies, and party benefactors, a considerable scandal at the time.

passed about. . . . Their houses commonly be very gallant . . .   *147*
within as white as milk, in such sort that it seemeth to be bur-
nished paper. The floors are paved with square stones, very
broad and smooth; their ceilings are of an excellent kind of
timber, very well wrought and painted, that it seemeth like
damask and of the color of gold. . . ." Literacy was widespread and the organization of society as impressive as the
architecture and urban engineering. Hospitals existed in
every city, "always full of people; we never saw any poor body
beg. We therefore asked the cause of all this; answered it was
that in every city there is a great circuit wherein be many
houses for poor people, for blind, lame, old folk, not able to
travel for age, nor having any other means to live. . . ." G. F.
Hudson, the eminent historian of the relations between
China and the West, writes that these accounts show "a society of enormous population and great material prosperity,
patriarchal in its essence, bureaucratically organized, stable
and immobile, expressing itself in stately ceremoniousness."

But even then the Spanish Jesuit Matteo Ricci also noted
that

[t]he power of China rests rather upon the great number of
towns and the multitude of inhabitants than upon the valour
of the people. . . . [T]he Chinese are accustomed to consider
their country as the centre of the world and to despise all
other nations. They are very much dreaded by all the kings
in the vicinity because they can assemble in a moment so
considerable a fleet that it frightens them by the number of
vessels; the Chinese are, however, but poor warriors, and the
military is one of the four conditions which are considered
mean among them. Nearly all the soldiers are malefactors
who have been condemned to perpetual slavery in the king's
service; they are fit only to war with thieves. . . .

A Spanish official in Macao annotated this report with the comment: "These vessels go out a little when it is fine weather, but hasten back at the least wind. They have some small iron guns, but none of bronze; their powder is bad . . . ; their arquebuses are so badly made that the ball would not pierce an ordinary cuirass. . . . With five thousand Spaniards, at the most, the conquest of this country might be made, or at least of the maritime provinces, which are the most important in the world. With half a dozen galleons and as many galleys one would be master of all the maritime provinces of China as well as of all that sea and the archipelago which extends from China to the Moluccas." Spain's war with England and the disaster of the Armada in 1588 distracted the Spanish from such an adventure; but others took over, and by the late nineteenth century had succeeded.

Even in the nineteenth century, China's resistance to Europe cannot be described as nationalist, since "national" consciousness still did not exist among the Chinese. The Chinese authorities tried simply to keep the Europeans confined to as few as possible points of contact: trading ports and segregated extraterritorial "concessions" where European law was allowed to prevail. This succeeded for a time, but the Opium Wars destroyed the authority and self-confidence of the imperial government. The English had found that opium, produced in India, could redress the trade deficit they experienced from their imports of Chinese silk, tea, and rhubarb (which was dried to make a drug and "tonic" prized in Europe), so they disregarded customs barriers and forced the drug onto Chinese markets. Opium's share of British exports to China went from 17 percent to 50 percent between 1818 and 1833, even though the trade had been prohibited by

imperial decree since 1729. Eventually the British went to war *149*
with China to impose the opium trade, annexing Hong Kong
and occupying Shanghai, obtaining five open "treaty ports."
Twelve years later the European powers (and the United
States) forcibly obtained another eleven treaty ports, free
navigation on the Yangtze, exemption of merchants from
Chinese law, broad immunities for missionaries, and other
privileges.

The popular reaction against this provoked the Anglo-
French punitive expedition to Peking of 1860, when the summer palace was burned, the emperor was required to
apologize to the Europeans for having caused them this
strenuous inconvenience, and China was compelled to pay
indemnities. The western powers were back in Peking in
1900 to put down the Boxers, looting the city. The American
general Adna Chaffee observed, "It is safe that where one real
Boxer has been killed since the capture of Peking, fifteen
harmless coolies or laborers on the farms, including not a
few women and children, have been slain."

Out of this three-century experience a Chinese national
consciousness emerged, itself based on western ideas. After
the First World War, Chen Tu-hsiu, the dean of the College
of Letters at the National Peking University and a leader of
the New Tide movement for intellectual emancipation in
China, wrote: "Whether in politics, scholarship, morality or
literature, the Western method and the Chinese method are
two absolutely different things and can in no way be compromised or reconciled. We need not now discuss which is better
and which is worse, as that is a separate issue. . . . But if we
decide to reform, then we must adopt the new Western
method in all things and need not confuse the issue by such

150 nonsense as 'national heritage' or 'special circumstances.' "
Out of this thinking came foundation of the Chinese Communist party.

When the hapless Manchus abdicated in 1911, it was Sun
Yat-sen, a Hawaiian-educated Christian much influenced by
western thought, who came to power. His Kuomintang—National People's party—struggled unsuccessfully through the
1920s and into the 1940s to unify the country and impose a
new central authority on territorial warlords. Its leaders were
increasingly influenced by Leninism as well as by Christianity, and then by Fascism. Sun called for help from the Comintern in 1924, but his successor, Chiang Kai-shek, broke
with Mao Tse-tung in 1927. The latter eventually won the
struggle between the Kuomintang and Communist movements (and doctrines) of national mobilization, both European in intellectual origin, although Mao's success came only
after he had rethought and restructured Marxism-Leninism
in order to make China's Communism a peasant-based
movement, adapted to the conditions and historical experience of Chinese society. Under the Communists, China
again became a unified state, ostensibly guided by the western "science" of dialectical materialism, while actually becoming a reconstituted dynastic polity in which Mao
Tse-tung assumed the godlike role of "great teacher" and
quasi-emperor (as his satellite, Kim Il Sung, today remains in
North Korea)—emperor of an ephemeral dynasty, history no
doubt will demonstrate. His Communist dynasty, proclaimed only in 1949, already approaches its end, the political
sequel unknown.

But China itself is no longer an isolated or self-sufficient
civilization. The mobilizing national ideology is founded on
the writings of a Rhineland Jewish scholar-journalist, himself

concerned with the plight of the European industrial working class, a social group which did not exist in Asia at the
time of China's revolution. China's present economic doctrines are borrowed from Adam Smith—and Ronald Reagan.
The country has become a nation among nations. Its wars
against the American-led UN coalition in Korea, against India in 1962, and against its Communist rival, Vietnam, in the
early 1970s were wars of national interest and territorial defense or aggrandizement. The war against the Tibetans' revolt in 1959–1960 was reconquest of a former tributary,
followed by an attempt to crush Tibetan religion and culture—and Tibetan nationalism.

The societies on the periphery of the great imperial civilization of China, Vietnam, Korea, and Japan, were always
nearer in character to the modern nation than China itself.
They could not be complacent vis-à-vis China, and had to be
aware of their precariousness and their need for collective
self-definition and self-defense. Japan, Korea, and Vietnam,
as modern nations, are the products of a militant resistance
to the cultural as well as political and military power of
China. Because they were apart from the imperial civilization and politically endangered by it, they were from the
start forced into a certain "national" mobilization to assert
and defend their particularity. The Tonkinese separated
themselves from the southern Chinese in the ninth century
of our era by means of a strenuous effort of self-assertion, in
time becoming a distinct society as well as an independent
kingdom. China's late-eighteenth-century emperor Ch'ien-
lung said, "The Vietnamese are indeed not a reliable people.
An occupation does not last very long before they raise their
arms against us and expel us from their country. The history

152 of past dynasties has proved this fact." They mounted the
same resistance in the twentieth century to French and
American power, and in addition had once again to defend
themselves against China.

Arnold Toynbee has written of these cultures at the edge
of great civilizations, which acquire an energy the central
civilization lacks. He says that a society on the rim of a great
and original civilization confronts a primordial challenge
"implicit in the relation itself, which begins with a differenti-
ation and culminates in a secession." The secession comes
when the original civilization has lost the creative allure
which previously had commanded the voluntary allegiance of
the border peoples. The nineteenth-century industrialization and modernization of Japan, and the equivalent development since the 1950s in South Korea and other small states of
essentially Sinic culture on the frontiers of China—Hong
Kong, Singapore, Taiwan—must be seen as their ultimate
self-defining secession from a preindustrial or early-indus-
trial Chinese civilization which had lost its magnetism, a loss
evident in the Manchu dynasty's nineteenth-century
foundering, confirmed by the twentieth-century failure of
both Nationalist and Maoist revolutions.

Conquest by non-Asian civilizations was a radical shock
to Asia's elites. Nothing in their own history had prepared
them for such a possibility, and it generated an entirely new
consciousness of themselves. They were compelled to see
themselves for the first time as part of a plurality of societies
rather than as unique, and as vulnerable. They were challenged to mobilize and defend themselves. It was impossible
for them to survive without change. Mobilization itself
changed them. It restored self-esteem and a sense of collec-

tive values. But this came only after Asians had experienced
the shame of conquest and domination, and had been forced
to adopt western political ideas and systems, and western
technologies, in order to reclaim their independence. The
cultural crisis this produced is far from over even now. The
victims of European imperialism discovered their vulnerability to dangers they had not before imagined could exist, their
original confidence in their completeness and superiority
derailed by the discovery of something radically different—
an alternative civilization determined, by its political-mili-
tary expansion into Asia, to teach Chinese, Indians, and all
other Asians that their fundamental values, and assumptions
about existence itself, were wrong and had to be replaced.

The West's Christian missionaries went to Asia determined to demonstrate that Asian philosophies were wrong,
that Asian religions were blasphemous, and that Asians must
worship the unique and omnipotent God known to the Europeans. These missionaries' twentieth-century secular counterparts, whether agents of the World Bank or the
International Monetary Fund, or American soldiers fighting
to impose an American political solution upon Vietnam (or
Cambodia), have been equally convinced of the superiority
of western political and economic ideas, and equally determined that they be adopted by Asians.

The consequences of the twentieth-century breakup of
the Dutch, Spanish, Portuguese, French, and British external
empires have been no less painful than those of the internal
collapse of the Hapsburg and Ottoman systems. International relations from the mid-1950s forward have been dis-
rupted and at times dominated by the conflict between
radicalized national or ideological movements in Asia and

154   governments in the West. While these Asian movements
have often been interpreted by the West as the product of international Communist influence and as threats to a democratic international order conceived in western terms, the
western powers have in fact been at war with the nationalism
of the region, a political and military mobilization of the
same forces of cultural resistance that produced the anti-
colonial uprisings of the nineteenth century.

The Soviet Union at the same time viewed the non-
western world as an arena for the expansion of "socialist"
power by means of political and military interventions in
support of "progressive forces." Like the West, it found itself
checked by a nationalism which either captured and diverted
to national purposes the Asian Communist movements, as in
China and Vietnam, or directly defied and defeated the Soviet intervention, as in Afghanistan. In Moscow as well as
Washington and the other western capitals, the popular fer-
vors and political struggles of these regions (and of Africa)
were nonetheless persistently given an irrelevant ideological
interpretation.

African nationalism enters only slightly into the present
discussion, since nationalism can scarcely be said to exist in
sub-Saharan Africa. National boundaries are those (except
for the borders of the ancient Ethiopian nation) decided by
the 1884–1885 Berlin conference of colonial powers, in general indifference to African ethnic and historical realities.
They remain unchanged today because the leaders of these
artificially defined states all recognize that an attempt to ra-
tionalize frontiers would produce chaos. Nonetheless, the attachments of Africans remain those of family, community,
tribe, ethnic group, and religion, not nation; although as ur-

banization continues, alienation from those attachments in- *155*
creases, with sober implications for the future. Even South
Africa's African National Congress, the closest there is to a
modern national movement in Africa, has its basis in a tribe,
the Xhosa. The "liberation movements" which were part of
the end of colonialism in the 1960s and 1970s were the creations of westernized elites. They mobilized a popular anti-
colonialism which, as in nineteenth-century Asia, was caused
by the cultural distress produced by the European presence
and European control, and by manifest social injustices, such
as expulsion from traditional lands (the case of the Kikuyu in
Kenya at the time of the Mau Mau uprising), forced labor,
economic exploitation generally, and invidious legal and administrative discrimination and segregation.

The new elites of the new African nations governed
unsophisticated and illiterate populations, agricultural or
pastoral peoples living at levels of social and economic development that had characterized Northern Europe centuries
earlier. This was backwardness by the criteria of social, economic, and political development imposed by contemporary
civilization, the criteria by which Africa's elites chose to measure themselves, and which they demanded be met in their
countries.

The observation that today's independent African governments are generally inferior to the white-dominated colonial governments which preceded them is taken by the
politically conformist as an argument that Africans (and
Asians, or some Asians, or certain Asians and Africans) are
inferior to whites. That this does not logically follow makes
no difference to those who wish to make such an interpretation, or fear it. In this respect the comment made in 1853 by

156   Alexis de Tocqueville, about the "monstrous fatalism" of the theories of racial superiority and inferiority of his young compatriot Arthur de Gobineau, is relevant. "The consequence [of such theories] . . . is that of a vast limitation, if not a complete abolition, of human liberty. . . . I am sure that Julius Caesar, had he had the time, would have willingly written a book to prove that the savages he had met in Britain did not belong to the same race as the Romans, and that the latter were destined thus by nature to rule the world while the former were destined to vegetate in one of its corners." It is absurd to think that a minute African elite should in the few years since independence have been able to provide its countries with superior government, successful economies, and impartial justice. What professional qualifications or experience did the members of this elite possess? What resources to count on? What were the doctrines they took from Europe? Few nationalist militants were engineers or economists, or professional administrators. Closest to that were certain military revolutionaries, but armies provide a model of command administration exactly opposite that of open and accountable government. Kwame Nkrumah of Ghana was an English-educated lawyer, Jomo Kenyatta an anthropologist, Léopold Senghor a poet. Because of the political circumstances of the times, nearly all committed themselves to naive and unworkable ideas of state socialism and industry-led development. Such was the fashion on the European Left. Nearly all accepted the proposition that single-party rule was the correct method to obtain rapid economic and social development: in Europe, during their formative years, democracy was in disrepute. The dominant European ideology of the 1930s and 1940s was Fascism, that of the 1950s and 1960s Marxism. African leaders now profess democracy. No

other solution remains. But that too is going to fail, in most
places at least, because the civil society, civil culture, and enlightened middle class essential to democracy are not there.

History has terminated the European empires in Asia
and Africa. The insurrectionary movements that began in
the spontaneous resentments and resistance of colonial peoples to foreign occupation, foreign rule, foreign injustices,
and above all—if in deeply ambiguous ways—foreign values
became in the twentieth century a series of successful "national liberation struggles." Before, the people of the great
central African tropical forest, or the savannas of East Africa,
did not know that they belonged to nations. They knew religion, kin, tribe, race, place, but not nations. Europe brought
them nationalism and made them nations—or the simulacra
of nations. Basil Davidson, one of independent Africa's most
sympathetic historians, argues that a precolonial civil society
had existed in Africa but that it was "undermined and finally
brought down by the decades of alien rule after Africa's imperialist partition in the 1880s, leaving as it seemed no valid
structures for the future." In the period of decolonization, in
the 1950s and 1960s, "[t]he fifty or so states of the colonial
partition, each formed and governed as though their peoples
possessed no history of their own, became fifty or so nation-
states formed and governed on European models, chiefly the
models of Britain and France. Liberation thus produced its
own denial. Liberation has led to alienation. . . ." The outcome was a "modern tribalism" having little to do with traditional society, which "flourishes on disorder, is utterly
destructive of civil society, makes hay of morality, flouts the
rule of law." The misgovernment of the contemporary
African nations is part of a larger tragedy of Africa in the

158   twentieth century, which has nothing to do with the nationalism of modern Europe.

However, independence is what people wanted, and they
have been willing to struggle for it; and if they have become
worse off for it, that is another of the tragedies of history
which an optimistic philosophy has difficulty admitting. The
immediate future of Africa, including that of a majority-
ruled South Africa, is bleak, and it would be better if the international community would reimpose a form of paternalist
neocolonialism in most of Africa, unpalatable as that may
seem. The mechanism of the international mandate, employed by the League of Nations after the First World War,
might be revived. However, the mandated power today would
have to be the UN itself, rather than one or several outside
powers, as in the past, since the latter almost certainly would
prove as unacceptable to governments asked to accept the
mandate as to the people made the subject of it.

The costs of the ideologically misconceived struggle between the states of the Communist bloc and the United
States, conducted in Asia and Africa at the expense of Asians
and Africans, proved very considerable for those who initi-
ated it, but a true nationalism was inspired in places where
that had never before existed. The Soviet system was penulti-
mately shaken by the national struggle of the Afghans—
added to that of the East Europeans, who had never accepted
Soviet colonization. The major West European states had already been humiliated in their confrontations with Asian nationalism. The Netherlands and France attempted and failed
to reestablish colonial rule in the Dutch East Indies (Indonesia) and in Indochina in the 1940s and 1950s. The French
later fought, and failed, to keep Algeria a part of France. The

Europeans were politically defeated, in militarily ambiguous
circumstances, both at Suez in 1956—when Britain and France
tried to depose Egypt's president, Gamal Abdel Nasser, and
retake the nationalized Suez Canal—and in Algeria.

France ended its protectorates of Morocco and Tunisia
in 1956, in circumstances of mounting unrest there, and
when General Charles de Gaulle came back to power during
the Algerian crisis of 1958, France gave independence to its
sub-Saharan African colonies (on terms, except in Guinea,
that perpetuated a generally constructive French economic
and political influence). In 1960 the Belgian Congo was
abandoned to its fate, which proved tragic, as did that of formerly British Uganda under General Idi Amin, formerly
French Central Africa under the egregious "Emperor"
Bokassa, and American-sponsored (and -dominated) Liberia.
Britain suppressed the Mau Mau uprising in Kenya that began in 1952, but by the start of the 1960s Britain had concluded that it was politically expedient to give independence
to Kenya and to its other East African colonies. Other
British protectorates and client states "east of Suez" were renounced (largely for budgetary and other internal British political motives) by the Labour governments of the late 1960s.
Britain had won a war with Communist and ethnic Chinese
guerrillas in Malaya in the mid-1950s, but in 1963 gave that
country (and Singapore) independence.

By the mid-1960s no European power except Portugal
still had the heart for colonialism, even in places where ending it actually meant abandoning people to exploitation by
cruel and ignorant despots, or to genocidal tribal or ethnic
struggle producing famine and anarchy. Portugal fought until 1975 to keep Angola its colony, but the war eventually provoked radical military uprising in the home country, much as

160   France's struggle in Algeria had eventually caused insurrec-
      tionary violence inside France itself. The United States ex-
      perienced a comparable humiliation in its Vietnam defeat,
      followed in 1979 by the collapse of Iran's American-spon-
      sored Pahlavi dynasty, when a radically nationalist Moslem
      integrist movement forced the shah of Iran to flee his coun-
      try and took American diplomats hostage. Thus did the
      Asian and African victims of colonialism take a certain sweet
      revenge.

7 *American*

Nationalism

T he American nation is not like the others. Its nationalism is that of an ideological nation. Its history is separate. It accepts no comparison with others, and so it has been the most nationalistic of all the major nations. Not only politicians and public men but the people themselves constantly assert its superiority over all the others, as if the virtue of its Constitution were proof of permanent national success. As evidence of the latter has weakened—the country's actual leading rank, which did exist, being lost in recent years in nearly all but gross economic weight and military power—the national claims have become more strident.* And yet this nationalism of the United States is a relatively late development, of the last century and a half, in a country whose people originally gave their loyalties to the individual states, and were united nationally mainly by

---

*George Kennan speaks of "the flag-waving, the sententious oratory, the endless reminders of the country's greatness, the pious incantations of the oath of allegiance, and the hushed, pseudo-religious atmosphere of national ceremony. . . . the self-righteous intolerance towards those who decline to share in these various ritualistic enactments."

162   their commitment to a principle of government.

The powerful influence the United States has exercised upon the development of political society elsewhere during the nineteenth and twentieth centuries is the result of the fact that this nation—like the Latin American republics which followed—was a creation of political ideas. The United States was never a society which was already "there," but one which was deliberately made. Its population was (is) all immigrant, including those now described as "Native Americans," who are actually Asian in origin. Like most aboriginal peoples made the victims of European expansion, America's "Indians" have never become completely assimilated into the imposed civilization, yet they were too weak to compel the invaders to accommodate, culturally, to them.

The reason for the United States' existence is the principle and practice of self-government as set forth in the Declaration of Independence and the Constitution. In this the United States differs fundamentally from the states which preceded it. Its fellow English-speaking colonial nations, Canada, Australia, and New Zealand, have no ideological foundation. They exist because they were made to exist; they did not choose to exist (although they may yet declare an ideological independence; there is a republican movement in Australia, while Canada continues to look for a final definition of its identity). Because it was an act of principle and ideology, the American Revolution had a great influence upon the French Revolution which followed, which in turn was the principal influence on the Latin American revolutions of the nineteenth century, and on the creation of republics there.

In Spanish America the republican movement—the "liberation" movement—was transnational, while the actual po-

litical demarcation of the new republics was much along the
lines of what originally were the great Spanish colonial gov-
ernorships, so there was from the start a problem of authentic "nationality" among the nations thus created. This was,
and remains, the case in Central America, originally part of a
single Spanish captaincy-general. The Central American
states were subsequently annexed to the ephemeral Mexican
Empire of 1822–1823, and later subjected to repeated United
States interventions, which continued through the Reagan
and Bush administrations (the Nicaraguan and Salvadoran
interventions, the "Contras" affair, the invasion of Panama).
It is difficult to see Panama, El Salvador, Guatemala, Hon-
duras, and Costa Rica as wholly autonomous nations, which
Mexico, Brazil, and Argentina, on the other hand, unmistakably are. Yet in only apparent paradox, the Central Americans are intensely "nationalistic" vis à-vis the United States,
a consequence of their vulnerability to its interventions and
influence. Their nationalism is not the product of any conviction of national authenticity, superiority, or uniqueness,
but of weakness, the lack of firm national identity.

The impact of the United States on early-nineteenth-
century Europe and Latin America (and later on Asia) was
due chiefly, as Tocqueville wrote in 1848, to the American
people's demonstration that the principle of egalitarianism
could be realized and democracy successfully established.

Though it is no longer a question whether we shall have a
monarchy or a republic in France, we are yet to learn
whether we shall have a convulsed or a tranquil republic,
whether it shall be regular or irregular, pacific or warlike, liberal or oppressive, a republic that menaces the sacred rights
of property and family, or one that honors and protects them

164   both. It is a fearful problem, the solution of which concerns
not France alone but the whole civilized world. If we save
ourselves, we save at the same time all the nations which sur-
round us. If we perish, we shall cause all of them to perish
with us. According as democratic liberty or democratic
tyranny is established here, the destiny of the world will be
different. . . .

Now, this problem, which among us has but just been
proposed for solution, was solved by America more than sixty
years ago. The principle of the sovereignty of the people,
which we enthroned in France but yesterday, has there held
undivided sway for over sixty years. . . . [T]he people who
have made it the common source of all their laws have in-
creased continually in population, in territory, and in opu-
lence; and—consider it well—it is found to have been, during
that period, not only the most prosperous, but the most stable, of all the nations of the earth. While all the nations of
Europe have been devastated by war or torn by civil discord,
the American people alone in the civilized world have remained at peace. Almost all Europe was convulsed by revolutions; America has not had even a revolt. The republic there
has not been the assailant, but the guardian, of all vested
rights; the property of individuals has had better guarantees
there than in any other country of the world; anarchy has
there been as unknown as despotism.

Where else could we find greater causes of hope, or
more instructive lessons?

The American nation had come about by hazard, and for
many years its quality as a single nation was in doubt. An
overseas colonial population, considering itself invidiously
subjected to a distant monarch and sovereignty, had objected
to being taxed while without representation in the government that imposed the taxes. From that came a rebellion with
a principled justification which articulated the great political

ideas of the age, those of the European Enlightenment: that   *165*
men are equal and that the purpose of government is to secure men's "inalienable" rights by obtaining the consent of
the governed in their governance. But it was, as Herbert Levi
Osgood of Columbia University wrote early in this century,
"apparently an act of the utmost recklessness. The people
were by no means a unit in its support, and in several of the
states widespread indifference to [the Declaration of Inde-
pendence], or active sympathy with the British, prevailed. In
New York, South Carolina and Georgia a condition of civil
war came sooner or later to exist." The American idea was a
radical one in its time and continues today to have radical
implications, including some which remain less than fully
grasped in the United States itself.

However, this experience, fundamental as it was for the
contemporary West, exempted the American nation from
full participation in a larger international history after 1783,
since the United States was, in a fundamental sense, fulfilled
at its start. Nothing that has followed has been thought really
to augment or alter the order created by the ratification of
the United States Constitution. The Constitution itself has
had only to be defended and interpreted, the nation it governs defended against internal division and external threat.
Thus a profound and increasingly immobilizing political
conservatism has coexisted with enormous change in society
and economy.

The circumstances of the eighteenth-century beginnings long ago vanished; yet the idea and ideals survive, preserved by their necessity to the United States' very existence
from subsequent reexamination. What originally was an Enlightenment, North European, white Protestant Christian
society with a formal commitment to a historically identifi-

166   able set of intellectual as well as political values has become
something quite different, not only as the result of the passage of historical time but increasingly as the consequence of
choices made: those of secularism and materialism, a market
test for values, a non-directive education, non-European immigration, and most recently (if tentatively) the effort to
adopt a multiculturalist and multiracialist social system—all
of them ideological choices. The fundamental ideological
commitment remains, detached from the culture of its origin—a fact less than reassuring when the future is considered.

In the beginning the United States was less a nation
than an uncertain confederacy of settlements distant from
one another, preoccupied by local interests, suffering the
great regional/moral curse of slavery. In 1800 there were a
recorded 5,308,483 persons in the United States, one fifth of
them black slaves. Each of these subsequently, for reasons of
congressional representation of the states in which they
lived, was given the grotesque standing of three fifths of a
free human being. Male, white, free adults numbered some
one million, and they conducted the affairs of the republic.
Most Americans lived on the Atlantic coast. Inland, beyond
the Alleghenies, something like five hundred thousand people had settled the wilderness and advanced the frontier,
confronting still-powerful Indian confederations, retreating
but intact societies allied with the British Canadians in the
North and the Spanish governors of West Florida and
Louisiana in the South.

Henry Adams (in his classic history of the Jefferson and
Madison administrations) wrote, "At the close of the eighteenth century nothing had occurred which warranted the
belief that even the material difficulties of America could be

removed." The American might brag of his national re- *167* sources of silver, copper, iron, and gold—still buried, but surely there—and of the fields in the West to be brought under cultivation, the cities to build, but Adams says that a foreigner could be forgiven for replying: "Gold! cities! cornfields! continents! Nothing of the sort! I see nothing but tremendous wastes, where sickly men and women are dying of home-sickness or are scalped by savages! mountain ranges a thousand miles long, with no means of getting to them, and nothing in them when you get there! swamps and forests choked with their own rotten ruins! . . ."

The great republican experiment was launched with ratification of the Constitution, but even Thomas Jefferson, the third president, was unsure that the new nation could survive as a single nation, nor was he fully convinced that it should. "Whether we will remain a confederacy," he wrote in 1804, "or form into Atlantic and Mississippi confederations, I believe not very important to the happiness of either part." He held that the legal basis of the association of the states was their power to withdraw at will.

Liberty was widely held to be dependent on the existence of an elite, and was thought by conservative Americans to be jeopardized by democracy, represented by the views of Thomas Jefferson. The French Revolution was taken as proof of the proposition that democracy results in tyranny. The Bostonian Fisher Ames wrote in 1803, "Our country is too big for union, too sordid for patriotism, too democratic for liberty. What is to become of it, he who made it best knows. Its vice will govern it, by practicing upon its folly. This is ordained for democracies." George Cabot, of the Cabots to whom the Lowells talked and who themselves

168   talked only to God, said that error was ineradicable even in
New England, where there was "more wisdom and virtue
than in any other part of the United States. . . . I hold
democracy in its natural operations to be government of the
worst." Only if governing power were restricted to the prop-
ertied classes was there the possibility of containing popular
emotionalism, ignorance, and criminality—or so it was held.

    The election of Jefferson in 1800 was thus taken to be a
victory for revolution. Jefferson himself was convinced that
he had confronted an attempt to reestablish monarchy in the
United States. Looking back, in 1818, he wrote that "a short
review of the facts . . . will shew that the contests of that day
were contests of principle, between the advocates of republican, and those of kingly government, and that, had not the
former made the efforts they did, our government would
have been, even at this early day, a very different thing from
what the successful issue of those efforts have made it." The
problem still was national unity, the creation of a true nation.
He went on:

>   The alliance between the states under the old articles of
> confederation, for the purpose of joint defence against the
> aggression of Great Britin [sic], was found insufficient, as
> treaties of alliance generally are, to enforce compliance with
> their mutual stipulations: and these, once fulfilled, that bond
> was to expire of itself, & each state to become sovereign and
> independent in all things. Yet it could not but occur to every
> one that these separate independencies, like the petty States
> of Greece, would be eternally at war with each other, &
> would become at length the mere partisans & satellites of the
> leading powers of Europe. All then must have looked forward
> to some further bond of union, which would insure internal
> peace, and a political system of our own, independent of that
> of Europe. Whether all should be consolidated into a single

government, or each remain independent as to internal mat- 169
ters, and the whole form a single nation as to what was foreign only, and whether that national government should be a
monarchy or republic, would of course divide opinions according to the constitutions, the habits, and the circumstances of each individual.

The War of 1812 moved the United States towards single nationhood but still did not produce a fully confirmed
nation. It was at bottom an affair provoked by the overseas
ramifications of Britain's struggle against revolutionary and
Napoleonic France. When war came, there were American
expansionists who imagined taking Canada at a blow, with
Britain distracted elsewhere, but the battles proved largely to
be fiascoes for the United States, which had its capitol and
the White House burned by a British expedition. The American troops invading Canada were defeated by a smaller
Canadian force at the Battle of Detroit. No more than ten
thousand Americans volunteered to fight in the war, in a
population of seven million. The militia served much as it
pleased, going home when that was convenient, and in the
East the militia often refused to fight at all. At Niagara, another American attack on Canada was stopped by the refusal
of the New York militia to cross the border. Only there, and
in Washington and on the frontiers of Ohio and Indiana, was
the daily life of Americans seriously perturbed.

The interest of most was to strengthen one state or section at the expense of others. The Virginia-born Tennessean
Felix Grundy, elected to Congress in 1811 expressly as a war
advocate, explained his ambition as not only to drive the
British from the continent and "receive the Canadians as
adopted brethren," but by so doing to weaken the power of
the northern states and promote that of the South. "This

170   war, if carried out successfully . . . will have beneficial political effects; it will preserve the equilibrium of the government. When Louisiana shall be fully peopled, the Northern
States will lose their power; they will be at the discretion of
others; they can be depressed at pleasure, and then this
Union might be endangered. I therefore feel anxious not
only to add the Floridas to the South, but the Canadas to the
North of this empire." The idea of federal union among the
states had not yet convinced the political class, whose loyalties remained chiefly regional. When Andrew Jackson,
whose party had previously been the bulwark of state sovereignty, said during his first term (1829–1833) that "disunion
by armed force is treason," he was accused of "Caesarism."

The Civil War ended the period in which the United
States remained a confederation of states of autonomous and
competitive powers, turning it into a federal union, centrally
governed—a nation. The South had as its fateful motive to se-
cede the preservation of slavery, although this was not the
only one of its motives, but it also believed itself to be acting
within the terms of the original agreement among the
colonies, which it understood to be a voluntary association of
states of equal and independent powers. In January 1861, after
the election of Abraham Lincoln to the presidency and the
subsequent secession of South Carolina, Mississippi, Florida,
and Alabama, Jefferson Davis of Mississippi, who was to become the president of the Confederacy, but who had long
doubted the wisdom of southern secession, said to the Senate,

Under these circumstances, of course, my functions termi-
nate here. . . . We but tread in the paths of our fathers when
we proclaim our independence and take the hazard . . . not in

hostility to others, not to injure any section of the country,   *171*
not even for our own pecuniary benefit, but from the high
and solemn motive of defending and protecting the rights we
inherited, and which it is our duty to transmit unshorn to our
children. . . . [W]hatever of offense there has been [here] to
me, I leave here. I carry with me no hostile remem-
brance. . . . Mr. President and Senators, having made the an-
nouncement which the occasion seemed to me to require, it
remains only for me to bid you a final adieu.

The southern states did not, of course, go in peace.
Abraham Lincoln, who had more or less blundered into the
Republican nomination, won the presidential election of
1860—by a plurality, against three opponents—on the issues
of opposition to slavery and preservation of the Union. He
had said in the first of his debates with Stephen A. Douglas,
in October 1854, four years before the great Lincoln-Dou-
glas debates of the Illinois senatorial election of 1858:

The doctrine of self-government is right, absolutely and
eternally right; but it has no just application, as here attempted. Or perhaps I should rather say that whether it has
such just application depends on whether a Negro is not or is
a man. If he is not a man, why in that case he who is a man
may, as a matter of self-government, do just as he pleases
with him. But if the Negro is a man, is it not to that extent a
total destruction of self-government to say that he too shall
not govern himself? When the white man governs himself,
that is self-government; but when he governs himself and
also governs another man, that is more than self-government; that is despotism. If the Negro is a man, why then my
ancient faith teaches me that "all men are created equal," and
that there can be no moral right in connection with one
man's making a slave of another.

•

172   The purpose of the war, for the North, was to prevent the southern states' secession, which is to say, to destroy their "national" existence, imposing federal supremacy upon them; and this was successfully done. The result defined an American nation—the nation as Lincoln saw it. His early speeches in Washington are revealing. James M. McPherson has drawn attention to the fact that in his first message to Congress in 1861, Lincoln employed the term *the Union* thirty-two times and *the nation* three times. In his Gettysburg Address of 1863, he used *nation* five times and *Union* not at all. In his second inaugural, in 1865, he said that the war had resulted from the one side's attempt to dissolve the Union, while the other side had fought to preserve the nation.

Gore Vidal has argued that the united nation thus created deserves a less sentimental consideration than it usually is given. "In a sense, we have had three republics. The first, a loose confederation of former British colonies, lasted from 1776 to 1789 when the first Congress under the Constitution met. The second republic ended April 9, 1865, with the South's surrender. In due course Lincoln's third republic was transformed (inevitably?) into the national security state where we have been locked up for forty years."

The alternative deserves thought. Had the Confederacy been allowed to go in peace, it seems hardly imaginable that slavery could have survived into the twentieth century. It would have had to be ended by the South itself (the moral cause usefully reinforced by the inevitable mechanization of southern agriculture). This might have produced a better aftermath than what actually happened: the bitter struggles of Reconstruction, with its scalawags and carpetbaggers, followed by the reimposition of black oppression through the mechanisms of Jim Crow. That lasted until the desegregation of the

United States army at the end of the 1940s and the civil rights legislation of the 1960s. These finally accorded the black population of the United States its legal equality with the white.

The political—or geopolitical—outcome of letting the Confederacy go would have been a North America composed of two medium-sized and one large but not gigantic nation. I myself am inclined to think this might have been a better outcome. North Americans today might be more comfortable with themselves and with the world. But this was not to be: Lincoln, Grant, Sherman, and the industrial production of the North decided otherwise. Contrary to the shibboleth, wars do settle things.

The North having imposed its will, the rhetoric of "states' rights" ignominiously survived in southern politics into the 1960s as a coded defense for a continuing institutionalization of racial segregation and discrimination, a contradiction of the war's supposed outcome. The actual "rights" of the states had disappeared in military defeat, and the legal tests subsequently made of the overriding power of the federal government served merely to confirm it. There were no more "sovereign" states in the United States of the kind which existed before 1861. Then Davis could say, "If I had thought that Mississippi was acting without sufficient provocation . . . I should still, under my theory of government, because of my allegiance to the State of which I am a citizen, have been bound by her action," and Robert E. Lee, who had no sympathy for either slavery or secession, nonetheless refused command of the Union's army, out of loyalty to his state of Virginia.

Nationalism in the United States before 1865 was attached to the states, above all to those where the southern

174   agrarian economy and a predominantly English and "Scotch-Irish" Calvinist (Arminian-Methodist*) religion had created a distinct American culture relatively unaffected by non-British-Celtic immigration elsewhere. Defeat and the humiliations, to the white population, of Reconstruction reinforced this southern nationalism, producing an embittered mythmaking that endured for the better part of the century which followed, but was never again politically decisive. The South was broken by the war of 1861–1865, an experience leaving it with a consciousness of failure and of tragedy the rest of the country never possessed.

There was even a community of exiles created, a diaspora of the unregenerate, who would not live under "Yankee domination." Some drifted further south, to Cuba and Central America. The well-to-do went to London or Paris. The contemporary French-American novelist and diarist Julian Green, child of an expatriate Savannah family, writes of his mother, "She made of her sons and daughters the children of a nation which no longer existed but lived on in her heart. She cast over us the shadow of a tragedy which darkened for her even the clearest days. We were eternally the conquered but unreconciled—rebels, to employ a word dear to her." The banner of the Confederacy was framed in gold on the wall of the salon of their apartment on the Rue de Passy in Paris—"your flag. . . . Remember it. That and no other."

She could as well have been a Pole of the Partitions, or of the totalitarian diasporas, or a White Russian, or a Scot

---

*Jacobus Arminius (1560–1609) of the University of Leiden challenged the strict and arbitrary predestinarianism of Calvin with a doctrine of the compatibility of human freedom with divine sovereignty. This became the belief of Charles and John Wesley, and thus of American Methodism. Irresistible grace was held compatible with man's achieving his own good through self-discipline, hard work, self-reliance, and frugality.

across the waters, follower of a maladroit king. The voracious standardizing and leveling machinery of modern American mass civilization has since obliterated most of the specificities of her Virginia and Georgia, and of the larger South even of the 1940s and 1950s—violent and evangelical, race- and religion-haunted, now mostly gone Snopes, to beer and moneymaking and a vulgar patriotism. The regional culture is gone, and with it the mad romanticism, the aggressive defense of honor. What remains? Faulkner's scent of verbena? That of the spring's gardenia in a schoolgirl's hair? A national literature—a memory—survives.

The regional "nationalism" which was powerful enough to send the South into rebellion and convulse the United States in the first great industrialized war, whose horrors in the Battles of the Wilderness, and Sherman's dispassionately ruthless march through Georgia, foreshadowed those of 1914–1918, was tamed by the 1960s. Southerners now were the loudest in shouting the united nation's claim to be "number one" in the world, the assertion which marked America's troubled progress through the Vietnam defeat, Middle Eastern terrorism, Central American invasions and interventions, and the country's confrontations with radical Islam during the 1970s and 1980s.

The nationalism of the new United States, after the Civil War, was fed by the great immigration of the mid-nineteenth century and after. The immigrants came to an American nation, to its opening northwestern and western territories, not to individual states, about which they knew next to nothing before they arrived. There were one hundred thousand immigrants in 1842; a quarter of a million in 1847; nearly a half million in 1850; two and a quarter million be-

176 tween 1847 and 1854. The new railroads not only opened the country west of the Mississippi and Missouri rivers but gave the country a continental conception of itself. Nebraska, Kansas, interior Iowa, Minnesota, and the Dakotas were settled in the years after the Civil War. The federally subsidized transcontinental railroad was completed in 1869, the Golden Spike driven near Ogden, Utah, on May 10, joining Council Bluffs, Iowa, on the Missouri River, to Sacramento and San Francisco. In the 1880s the Northern Pacific and the Great Northern railways opened the Northwest, and the Santa Fe and Denver & Rio Grande the Southwest. The West of American myth, of the open range and cattle drives and range wars, lasted from the early 1870s to the mid-1880s. The first congressional use of the words *manifest destiny* was in connection with the settlement of Oregon, an expression, as the historian Frederick Jackson Turner said, of the American people's belief in their destiny and "right" to "spread over this whole continent."

Continental domination was also an idea behind the ultimatum to France in 1866 demanding French withdrawal from Mexico. Preoccupation with a Pacific destiny for the United States existed even then, in part the result of fears generated by Chinese migration to California. Demand for a Central American canal connecting the Atlantic and Pacific began in the 1860s. The state of Panama was invented by the United States in 1903, to make possible a canal's construction, under U.S. authority, in that new and allegedly sovereign territory. The canal was opened in 1914 and dedicated in 1920. The concern with the Pacific also brought about the occupation and annexation of the Midway Islands in 1867 and acquisition of coaling stations for the American navy in the Samoan and Hawaiian islands.

In 1886 Captain Alfred Thayer Mahan delivered a series of lectures to officers at the new Naval War College in Newport, Rhode Island, which four years later were published as *The Influence of Sea Power upon History*, a work of immense influence in turning the United States from continental to Pacific empire. Mahan said that national security no longer lay in continental defense and isolation but in the possession of colonies and the protection of the sea-lanes by which international commerce was conducted. "It seems demonstrable . . . that as commerce is the engrossing and predominant interest of the world today, so, in consequence of its acquired expansion, overseas commerce, overseas political acquisition, and maritime commercial routes are now the primary objects of external policy among nations. The instrument for the maintenance of policy directed upon these objects is the navy. . . ." He also said that national expansion took place through "no premeditated contrivance of our own"; it was "natural, necessary, irrepressible."

Mahan was the principal intellectual influence on the development of the new American will to empire. This exploded upon the Spanish Empire in 1898, destroying it overnight, inflicting what became known in Spanish history as "the Disaster," taking over Spain's principal possessions in the Caribbean and the Pacific Ocean: Cuba, Puerto Rico, Wake Island, and the Philippine Islands. Hawaii was annexed as well. President William McKinley, who in his inaugural address the year before had said, "We want no war of conquest; we must avoid the temptation of territorial aggression," in 1898 confronted the problem of the status of the Philippine Islands. According to his own account he fell to his knees to pray for guidance, and in the early hours of the

178   morning he heard the voice of God instructing him to annex the Philippines. When it came to Hawaii, McKinley concluded, "We need Hawaii just as much and a good deal more than we did California. It is manifest destiny."

The new American imperialism had another and simpler cause. The country boomed after the Civil War. Industry rapidly overtook that of Western Europe. There was little sympathy for the agrarian and Stoic values of the age of Jefferson and Washington. America of the "Gilded Age" wanted its place in the sun, and was prepared to buy it, as the daughters of its merchant and industrial barons bought titles from the aristocracies of England and the continent. The dominant historical philosophy was that of Social Darwinism, its assumptions plain in Theodore Roosevelt's claim that "in every instance [national] expansion [in Europe] has taken place because the race was a great race. It was a sign and proof of greatness in the expanding nation, and moreover bear in mind that in each instance it was of incalculable benefit to mankind. . . . When great nations fear to expand, shrink from expansion, it is because their greatness is coming to an end. Are we still in the prime of our lusty youth, still at the beginning of our glorious manhood, to sit down among outworn people, to take our place with the weak and craven? A thousand times no!" Spain's misfortune was that its colonies lay at hand, poorly defended.

Roosevelt's success was less as a political reformer than as a preacher of the manly and military virtues, which he felt were threatened by the materialism of an expanding commercial society. He said that the American "commercial classes are only too likely to regard everything merely from the standpoint of 'Does it pay?' and many a merchant does not take any part in politics because he is short-sighted

enough to think that it will pay him better to attend purely to 179
making money. . . . It is also unfortunately true . . . that the
general tendency among people of culture and high education has been to neglect and even to look down upon the
rougher and manlier virtues. . . ." He was just the man for
America's age of imperialism. Richard Hofstadter describes
his qualities as "romantic nationalism, disdain for materialis-
tic ends, worship of strength and the cult of personal leadership, the appeal to the intermediate elements of society, the
idea of standing above classes and class interests, a grandiose
sense of destiny, even a touch of racism." (These Hofstadter,
writing in 1948, identifies as also the qualities of "recent au-
thoritarianism," although they would seem mostly the qualities possessed by Winston Churchill and Charles de Gaulle.)

The new American nation's imperialism never really admitted that it was what it was, since Cuba and the Philippines
were ostensibly taken in order to liberate their inhabitants
(our "little brown brothers," in the contemporary phrase),
even though these inhabitants rapidly demonstrated their
wish to be free from the United States as well as from Spain.
American relations with Cuba ever afterwards were distinguished by Washington's insistence that all it did during its
persistent interventions was really only for the Cubans' best
interests, unmarred by selfish concerns (this goes on today).
Of the Philippines, Elihu Root, secretary of war from 1889 to
1904, and later secretary of state under the first Roosevelt
and recipient of the Nobel Peace Prize, said, "Government
does not depend on consent. The immutable laws of justice
and humanity require that a people shall have government,
that the weak shall be protected, that cruelty and lust shall be
restrained, whether there be consent or not. . . . There is no
Philippine people." It required a three-year war to pacify the

180   Philippine Islands, during which a quarter of a million died, only five thousand of them American soldiers. The resistance of the Moslems of Mindanao and the Sulu Archipelago, the "Moros," went on until 1916. Afterwards, the Filipinos were promised eventual independence—and given it in 1946. Hypocrisy was always the virtue of American imperialism.

The moralism in the American outlook made it more comfortable to substitute a reformist internationalism for the national expansionism of the imperialist period. Social Darwinism was a hard doctrine by which as many lost, and were cast down, as won. Woodrow Wilson's liberal internationalism provided an expression of that form of American nationalism more exactly described as national exceptionalism. This holds that American virtues are unparalleled elsewhere and represent a form of more perfect society which the rest of the world strives to attain.

American foreign policy under Wilson, and again after the Second World War, represented the attempt to extend to international society the values and institutions of the United States. This included that commitment to federal political organization which had been dominant in the country since the Civil War. Hence the distressed American reaction to any principled defense of nationalism elsewhere (as by de Gaulle).*

The immediate source of American exceptionalism was another nineteenth-century intellectual tendency, the devel-

*In 1991–1992, the U.S. government's policy towards the disintegrating Soviet Union and Yugoslavia was damagingly influenced by this conviction that for countries to break into their component parts was not only wrong but doomed to failure, since the "natural" and progressive tendency of political entities is to federate, evolving towards larger units—as the United States has done.

opment in American Protestant thought called the Social
Gospel. This held that man progressively overcomes evil as
human nature improves, and implied that in the United
States, because of the merit of its political institutions, human nature was being perfected at a more rapid pace than
elsewhere. Hence, an American duty existed to extend the
benefits of this system.

Frances FitzGerald's examination of the influence of
millenarian, or premillenarian, theology ("we are living in
the last days") on American politics says that while the millenarian view was to become very influential in the cold war
years ("absolute evil confronts us; if we do not prevail here
[in Vietnam, in Nicaragua, etc.] our defenses against disorder and evil everywhere will crumble"), the political Gnosti-
cism of the Social Gospel dominated the period from 1916 to
the cold war. It of course remains influential today. While it
was "as much a minority position as premillennialism among
[nineteenth-century American] Protestants, . . . the general
strain of thinking was quite widespread. Woodrow Wilson
went to the Paris Peace Conference with the Gnostic vision
that the United States could bring peace, freedom, and justice to the world by an act of will. During and after World
War II it was this vision which filled the rhetorical sails of a
great many public figures from Roosevelt to Wendell Willkie
to Henry Luce."

It is a view which has been announced in American policy discourse ever since. The erection of a replica of the
Statue of Liberty in Tiananmen Square in Beijing in 1989 was
taken in the United States as still another confirmation that,
as Tom Paine put it in *Common Sense*, the American cause is
"the cause of all mankind." During the Reagan and Bush administrations it was commonly argued that the wish of all the

182   rest of the world to emulate the United States was demonstrated by the fact that there was a vast demand to emigrate to
the United States. This did not acknowledge that the principal motive for emigration is poverty and political oppression
in the country of emigration, and that the choice of where to
go is usually decided by where people can get to, and who will
take them in. The American triumphalism of the Gnostic period contrasted notably with the modesty of an earlier time,
when Lincoln prayed humbly that the nation might find itself
doing God's will.

As a neutral power during the first two years of the First
World War, the United States considered itself uniquely
above the struggle, morally different, "the Great Neutral,"
conserver of sane and just peacetime values and the exponent
of "peace without victory." *The Wabash Plain Dealer* said in
1914, "We never appreciated so keenly as now the foresight
exercised by our forefathers in migrating from Europe."
However, this conviction of American moral superiority and
distance was by 1917 transformed into a campaign to crush
"the military masters of Germany" by means of the War
That Would End War. The United States now was held not
only to possess superior motives to those of its allies, but to
have a moral commission to reform Europe. This was responsible for the tragedy which followed. Richard Hofstadter
writes that when Wilson went to the peace conference at
Versailles,

[w]hat he really wanted was not simply a "peace without victory," but a victory to be followed by an unvictorious peace.
He wanted the Allies and Germany to come to the conference table as victors and vanquished and sit down as negotia-

tors. Events soon impressed upon him the impossibility of any such thing. He told one of the American experts who accompanied him to Paris that "we would be the only disinterested people at the Peace Conference, and that the men whom we were about to deal with did not represent their own people." The second statement was in some ways an unhappy delusion, but the first was true: the United States, thanks in part to Wilson's restraining influence, was the only nation among the victors that came without a set of strictly national aims, without a single claim for territory, indemnities, or spoils. . . . The Conference was an affair of three sides—the victors, the vanquished, and Wilson.

Wilson's belief that the other national leaders at the conference did not represent their own people expressed his conviction that it was he, as America's leader, who really represented them, since the fundamental values and general interests of mankind were those already achieved or fulfilled in the United States, to whose condition the others logically aspired.

This was the higher American nationalism of the Wilson period, which has prevailed again ever since the Second World War. Both the League of Nations and the UN have been programs for reorganizing international society according to the values of the United States. George Kennan summarized Wilson's ambition in this way: the League "would mobilize the conscience and power of mankind against aggression. Autocratic government would be done away with. Peoples would themselves choose the sovereignty under which they wished to reside. Poland would achieve her independence, as would likewise the restless peoples of the Austro-Hungarian Empire. There would be open diplomacy this time; peoples, not governments, would run things. Ar-

184 maments would be reduced by mutual agreement. The peace would be just and secure." The actual consequences were otherwise.

The higher nationalism was accompanied by a recrudescence of a lower nationalism. The trauma of the world war, and certainly that produced by America's sense of betrayal when the Russian Revolution turned into the Bolshevik Revolution, produced a wave of nativism, chauvinism, and racism in the months following the armistice. This was connected to the belief that foreign Communism and anarchism threatened the country. The American people's relationship to revolution has always been difficult and ambiguous, and the Bolshevik coup in Moscow was a shock to American preconceptions. In the eighteenth century there had been a serious debate over whether the country should go to war to support the French Revolution, initially taken to be an imitation of the American Revolution. Later, the administration of John Adams praised the Haitian Revolution and Toussaint L'Ouverture, signed a treaty with him, and provided arms and provisions for his army. As in the French case, interest lapsed when it was apparent that what was going on had little resemblance to the American experience.

In 1917, the February Revolution was similarly welcomed. Seven days after the czar abdicated, the United States recognized the new Russian government of Aleksandr Kerensky. It was the first country to do so. President Wilson declared that Russia now was "a fit partner for a league of honor" and the American ambassador in Saint Petersburg said that he expected the revolution to produce "a republic, and with a government . . . founded in correct principles." But then the Bolsheviks seized power and declared that their

revolution had nothing at all to do with anything that had
gone before, but was a totally new departure in world history.
This time the United States was the last major power to recognize the new government. American hostility towards the
Bolsheviks, as Gordon S. Wood has written, had very much
to do with the fact that the Soviet Union "threatened nothing less than the displacement of the United States from the
vanguard of history. The Russians, not the Americans, now
claimed to be pointing the way toward the future (and more
alarming still, there were some Americans in the 1920s and
1930s who agreed with that claim)."

The answer to this problem was to decide that the Bolshevik Revolution was a false revolution, usurping true democratic revolution, the work of a self-interested conspiratorial
minority, which imposed itself by propaganda and subver-
sion—all of which was true enough. The same argument
subsequently was made about the Chinese, Cuban, and Vietnamese revolutions, and most of the other Third World
movements which rose against established powers in the
name of proletarian revolution or with the support of the Soviet Union, China, or Cuba. But the United States was increasingly isolated in arguing that it alone stood for true
revolutionary values.

The nativist nationalism that prevailed for a time after
the Great War expressed more than disillusionment at the
failure of American internationalist reform. There had always been a streak of straightforward nativism and exclusion-
ism in the United States, on the part of those who were
already Americans against those who were the latest to come.
The historian John Lukacs has described what happened in
the 1920s as the transformation of "Americanism" "from an

186   ideology of becoming [that of the assimilation of immi-
grants] into an ideology of being." What in another time was
patriotism became exclusionary and rhetorically aggressive.
The practice of playing the national anthem at sports and
school events, what Lukacs calls "the military bedecking and
panoply of high school parades," and the reciting of the
Pledge of Allegiance in schools, all were innovations of the
post-1919 period, as were the radical- and anarchist-hunting
"Palmer raids." A. Mitchell Palmer (known, if you will believe it, as "the fighting Quaker") was Wilson's attorney general. Convinced of the imminence of Bolshevik/anarchist
revolution, which was linked in the attorney general's mind
to trade unionism, on New Year's Eve 1920 he made use of
the wartime Sedition Act to seize for summary deportation
thousands of persons suspected of radical or revolutionary
activities. Six thousand eventually were arrested. Most
charges had to be dropped for lack of evidence, but the strident anti-foreignism reflected in Palmer's actions was to
mark the rest of the decade. Union organization was challenged, textbooks were censured, and racist, anti-Semitic,
and anti-Catholic campaigns prospered.

The Immigration Act of 1924 placed an overall limit on
immigration of 150,000 persons annually, imposing national
quotas linked to the existing national composition of the
United States. The revived Ku Klux Klan (an imitation of the
KKK of the Reconstruction period) had a few hundred members in 1920, and four and a half million by 1924. It became
for a time the dominant political power in Oregon, Okla-
homa, Texas, Arkansas, Indiana, Ohio, and California. Its
purpose was "to unite white male persons, native-born Gen-
tile citizens of the United States of America, who owe no allegiance of any nature to any foreign government, nation,

institution, sect, ruler, person or people . . . to maintain forever white supremacy . . . [and] conserve, protect, and maintain the distinctive institutions, rights, privileges, principles,
traditions and ideals of a pure Americanism."

This nativism and populist xenophobia in the
post–Great War period resembled the McCarthyism of the
1950s, when the country again was convulsed by a search for
supposed subversives (often a distraction from the search for
real ones, of whom, in the not entirely faded glow of western
liberal enthusiasm for the Russian Revolution, there were
some—usually poor and idealistic, like the eventually elec-
trocuted Soviet spies, Ethel and Julius Rosenberg). There
was a difference, however. The nativist nationalism of the
earlier period flourished among working-class Anglo-Saxon/
Celtic Protestants, the original stock of the country, who believed themselves threatened by Catholic and Jewish South
and East European immigration. McCarthyism was a phenomenon of recently assimilated immigrants, more often
than not Catholics, intent on demonstrating that the purity
of their "Americanism" was superior to that of the old-estab-
lished but liberal and cosmopolitan Anglophile Protestants.
Thus the State Department—held to have "lost China," and
to be responsible for other postwar inconveniences as well—
was a principal object of McCarthyist attack, together with
the established institutions of eastern private education, the
eastern press, and public service. The ideological nature of
American citizenship was again evident in the contention
that these people and groups practiced "un-American" activities. Un-French or un-Swedish activities are inconceivable,
since Frenchness and Swedishness are conditions, not political commitments.

188   This kind of exclusionary nationalism was nothing new in the 1920s or 1950s. The United States had its "Know-Nothing" movement in the mid-nineteenth century, which was anti-immigrant and anti-Catholic (its members invariably said they "knew nothing" when asked about the movement's leaders and exact programs). There was much anti-oriental agitation in the later nineteenth century (producing the Immigration Act of 1882, which excluded immigrants from East Asia). All of this represented a defensiveness about the American nation and its status in an international society still dominated by the European great powers, European intellectual life, and European manners.

The period of defensive nationalism of the United States ended with the Second World War. What followed was a different phenomenon, neither isolationist nor xenophobic, but liberal and internationalist, and also, increasingly, ideological. Some saw the new totalitarian challenge in metaphysical terms. The formidable, if formidably wrong, James Burnham, a one-time Trotskyist and later the intellectual progenitor of American neoconservatism, wrote in the winter 1944–1945 issue of the *Partisan Review* that Soviet power,

like the reality of the One of Neo-Platonism . . . flows outward, west into Europe, south into the Near East, east into China, already lapping the shores of the Atlantic, the Yellow and China Seas, the Mediterranean, and the Persian Gulf. As the undifferentiated One, in its progression, descends through the stages of Mind, Soul and Matter, and then through its fatal Return back to itself; so does the Soviet power, emanating from the integrally totalitarian center, proceed outward by Absorption (the Baltics, Bessarabia, Bukovina, East Poland), Domination (Finland, the Balkans,

Mongolia, North China, and tomorrow Germany), Orient-
ing Influence (Italy, France, Turkey, Iran, central and south
China . . .), until it is dissipated in MH ON, the outer material sphere, beyond the Eurasian boundaries, of momentary
Appeasement and Infiltration (England, the United States).

A metaphysical challenge suited Americans of the 1940s and
afterwards right down to the ground. It was Freedom against
Evil. The metaphysical language lasted in presidential
speeches certainly through the terms of Ronald Reagan and
George Bush.

The period from the 1950s to the end of the cold war
saw a sharp decline in the influence of mainstream religion
as well as an increasing Asian immigration, for which the
conventions and symbols of traditional American nationhood were alien, so that Lukacs remarks "that nationalism,
with its symbols and its functional rhetoric, may be the only
religion that masses of otherwise inchoate Americans have in
common." The Second World War had produced a great
popular uprooting, and the postwar economic transformation of the country entailed the effective loss of the nation's
regional identities, which had been crucial to its historical
development, anchoring Americans in given places and in a
solid complacence about what happened elsewhere. As late as
the 1940s the South still existed as a region and distinct culture, with a vigorous and original literature, still in some
sense a nation itself. This was ended by the physical and social change, the mobilization and mobility, imposed by the
war and the postwar economy. The rival New England regional civilization of which Henry Adams was representative—"I belong to the class of people who have great faith in
this country and who believe that in another century it will
be saying in its turn the last word of civilization"—had waned

190 long before the First World War. The distinctive New England high culture had faded from a ferocious Calvinism to Unitarianism, Transcendentalism, and into pale Christian Science. New England literature was finished by the time of the expatriation of Henry James and the death of Henry Adams. In mid-twentieth-century America only the easterner Edmund Wilson, of New Jersey and New York State, persevered with a major literary and intellectual enterprise conducted outside the stultifying and self-referencing academy. Midwestern regionalism, as an intellectual and literary phenomenon, was a brief affair—Willa Cather, Theodore Dreiser, Harriet Monroe, *Poetry, The Midland.* The major midwestern literary figures then and afterwards (except Nelson Algren) left for more cosmopolitan circumstances, which disappointed them.

The New England–New York governing class which dominated the financial and industrial institutions of the United States from the Civil War to the administration of Richard Nixon was destroyed as a political class by the Vietnam catastrophe—which it had been chiefly responsible for bringing about. Its members, occupying leading places in the Kennedy and Johnson administrations (as in those of their predecessors), had become convinced of the interlinkage of Vietnamese, Chinese, Cuban, and Soviet Communism with Third World radicalism, and were determined that, unlike their fathers (literally so, in some cases), they would not appease totalitarianism or sacrifice an ally, as had been done at Munich. Their failure to recognize the historical specificity of Vietnam in the 1960s, and their easy acceptance of an ideologized worldview, led the United States into a crisis from which it is fair to say it still has not emerged. Mr. Clinton became president in 1993 despite his having opposed the Viet-

nam War. George Bush was the last of what had been described as the Eastern Establishment to hold high power in
Washington: febrile inheritor of the legacy of Adamses and
Lodges and Quincys, victim of a new society where the marketplace determines values, even trying to pass himself off as
a Texan.

The old America was that of the original states and the
opening of the West. Immigrant America was an affair of establishing (not always successfully) new roots in urban ghettos and the neighborhoods and towns of the central states
and Middle West, where Swedetowns and Little Bohemias
came into existence, as well as German Milwaukee, Dutch
Pella in Iowa, Mennonite settlements and those of Pietist socialists (who, in Amana, in Iowa, turned to manufacturing
washing machines). There were German and Swedish
Lutheran seminary settlements, and German Benedictine—
even Trappist—priories and abbeys, Irish convent colleges,
expatriated French religious institutions (whence the University of Notre Dame du Lac, only in America capable of
becoming "the Fighting Irish"). They created a complicated
America, overwhelmingly religious, devoted to assimilation
and simplification. This was the America of the American
Dream, famously lost today except as it is preserved on cellu-
loid in those 1930s and 1940s films which were themselves
dreams of America, manufactured, as it has been said, by immigrant Jews in a Hollywood which was also a dream of
America, and is also lost today.

The contemporary United States was inaugurated by
the war in Vietnam, a product of liberal optimism and belief
in the universal relevance of American democratic values. Its
justification was the argument that the Communist move-

192 ment in South Vietnam was the agent of a deliberate and provocative policy of Chinese international aggression, meant to tip the balance of world power by mobilizing Third World radicalism, the "rural world," against the "urban world" of the western democratic powers.

The American government possessed full and sober confidence in its assumed mission to install democracy in Asia as rival to Communism, and few in Washington could imagine that the United States would not prevail. This intervention into Vietnam's national revolution clearly resembled the United States' imperial interventions into the Cuban and Philippine colonial uprisings of 1898. Its ambition was that of Wilson's crusade in 1917–1919. It reflected the same confidence in the relevance of American democracy to an Asia in upheaval that shaped Franklin Roosevelt's sponsorship of Kuomintang China as one of World War II's "Big Four," with a permanent UN Security Council seat and veto power bestowed upon it in 1945.

The Vietnam intervention was an expression of supreme American national confidence, at the zenith of a period when the United States was not only the world's most powerful economy and military power but the acknowledged "leader of the free world." The president, without ceasing to be the president of the United States, had in American belief become the president of international democracy, and of more. The West European nations and Japan not only acquiesced in this but solved important political problems of their own by becoming American satellites. American policy became their policy as well; resistance to this development was amazingly slight. (Only Charles de Gaulle made trouble, and even his position depended upon exploitation of the Soviet-American balance.) The Free World was not external to the United

States but an extension or radiation of the American nation.   *193*
American nationalism was thus an internationalist patriotism, or so it was seen by Americans.

However, the war failed. Vietnam was a defeat. To the
general confusion, the American people found themselves
not only frustrated in their prosecution of the military campaign but discovering that they were not unmistakably on the
side of virtue. The war the United States waged was more
and more stained by atrocity and terror, so that a kind of
dumb mutiny occurred inside the conscript army, and there
was a political revulsion in the country at what was happen-
ing, powerful enough to bring down two presidents and last-
ingly to divide and embitter American political society.

The national self-doubt which marked the United States
from the Vietnam crisis forward was a fear of wasted sub
stance and betrayed moral inheritance, with a seeming loss of
that capacity, or willingness (no doubt the same thing), to
work and sacrifice in common which had been the American
people's best quality in the past. The Reagan presidency was
an interlude of falsified renewal, in which the country's nationalism became almost frenzied, as the real threat to the
United States precipitously declined. The Soviet Union was
no longer a serious force, the palsied Leonid Brezhnev a
walking metaphor for the condition of his country, which
during the later Reagan years threw itself into the desperate
effort of reform that was to precipitate collapse. The United
States nonetheless treated the Soviet Union with exaggerated
alarm, and pursued surrogate "victories" over Grenada,
Libya, and Panama, which were accompanied by celebrations
of American might so hypertrophic in their triumphalism as
to bear blatant evidence to the nation's inner doubt. The re-

194   ality was that American military leadership no longer wanted any challenge without a guaranteed outcome, while the American people knew that the common life was getting worse, not better.

The era ended with the country deep in debt, faltering industrially, the individual living standard reduced, the prospect that of a future in which children lived less well than their fathers and mothers—and thus a contradiction of the primordial and defining national optimism. David Rieff has written that the country became one in which although the poor might revolt (as in the Los Angeles riots of spring 1992), "the middle class has done something far more radical: It has seceded, and it is difficult to see, barring some systemic collapse of the capitalist economy as a whole, how any reunion between the high-tech Spartans and the immiserated helots can be brought about." George Bush paid the political price for this in the presidential election of 1992, when William Jefferson Clinton assumed the responsibility of attempting to reverse the decline.

The old, expansive nationalism of the United States from 1898 to the zenith of the cold war rested on a belief in, and the accomplishment of, One from Many: the nation which was not a people, but a realized idea. "I think it is the most beautiful history in the world," Scott Fitzgerald wrote in a letter near the end of his life. "It is the history of all aspiration—not just the American dream but the human dream, and if I came at the end of it that too is a place in the line of the pioneers." But the nation in the 1990s was a different and more divided place than before, with its narcissism, its obsession with material gratifications and its falling educational standards, its new immigrations, and the still unresolved legacy of slavery evident in the black ghettos and the rhetoric and reality of racial hatred. Fitzgerald had also earlier observed that since the Civil War Americans had "substituted melodrama for tragedy, violence for dignity under suffering," and that proved a prophecy of the decades of the later cold war and its aftermath.

The fundamental questions remained open. An American nationalism exists which has shown itself capable of great altruism, and also of a vindictive violence against helpless enemies. The form it assumes in the future will follow from the internal settlement: whether there is success or a failure in reanimating the national idea, and thereby the nation's confidence. Without that, the undoubted strength of the country might be employed in a search outside itself for those reassurances it has failed to find within.

8 *Liberal Internationalism*

I have used the word *nationalism* in this book in its widest sense, and also in several senses. I have done so because what is called nationalism is an expression of the primordial attachments of an individual to a group, possessing both positive and destructive powers, and this is a phenomenon which existed long before the group to which such passionate loyalty was attached became the modern nation-state. The attachment exists in associations which have nothing to do with the nation-state (religion, obviously; the football team, trivially, but also significantly; the attachment may or may not have a rational basis). It may be understood as a form of love of self. It is also an expression of hope, a form of utopian expectation. It will certainly survive the replacement of the nation-state by any other form of political association—if that should occur.

Ethnic and communal conflict, and racial, religious, or linguistic rivalry and struggle, such as take place in India, Sri Lanka, or sub-Saharan Africa, or in Northern Ireland or Canada, or such as continues today between whites and blacks in the United States, all exist for reasons having nothing orig-

196

inally to do with nation-states. The griefs of tribal and religious struggle in Africa, or of the conflict between Hindus and Moslems in India, are not issues of nationalism, although the passions may be identical to those of nationalism. Nor is Islamic fundamentalism. The latter is capable of taking over national governments in the Moslem world and provoking policies exceedingly inconvenient to the western powers, as happened in Iran, but it remains a defensive and reactive phenomenon occurring in a civilization, and only coincidentally in a nation-state. It expresses that civilization's failure to compete on equal terms with the modern secular West. It looks for power over the Islamic states because the state is the vehicle of economic, technological, and military strength by which the Islamic militant can defend against the secularizing as well as the geopolitical influence of industrial society. It also is a movement which finally will exhaust itself, since it lacks the intellectual resources capable of giving the Islamic peoples what they want. Nationalism, on the other hand, is not something which will exhaust itself—not in our time.

Nationalism is the political (and military) expression of a form of group identity attached to an existing state, or to a community which is not yet a recognized nation-state but which believes that it should become one.* It can be a form of utopianism. The war which began in 1991 in the former Yu-

---

*Senator Daniel Patrick Moynihan says in his book *Pandaemonium* that a distinction exists between ethnic group and nation, between ethnicity and nationality, but that "[i]t is a distinction of degree. The nation is the 'highest' form of the ethnic group, denoting a subjective state of mind as regards ancestry, but also, almost always, an objective claim to forms of territorial autonomy ranging from a regional assembly to full-blown independence." This seems fair enough, so long as one understands that the ethnic nation is itself the exception among nations. Among the major powers of the present day, only Germany (which is not) and Japan (which is) consider themselves ethnic nations—which is a matter for reflection.

198 goslavia was not an irresistible cultural explosion out of an obscure or incomprehensible past, a volcanic event no one could have been expected to deflect.* It was motivated in part by a Serbian utopianism involving an idealized image of the past. Yet the conflict between Serbs and Croats is actually a modern affair, dating from the beginning of the present century, and connected with the general rise of European nationalisms. According to the historian Paul Garde,

The first real manifestation of hostility dates from 1902, when the Serbs, proud of the renaissance of their people, began to contest the separate existence of a distinct Croatian nation, and a Serbian journalist in Zagreb, Nikola Stojanovic, published an article with the provocative title, "Either Your Destruction or Ours," which caused anti-Serbian riots. Nevertheless a Serbian-Croatian coalition held a majority of seats in the Croatian parliament until the first world war. The gulf did not really open until 1918, when to their mutual unhappiness, the two people were united in a single state, the Yugoslav monarchy, where one of them, the Serbs, exercised an absolute domination, and the other was treated as a negligible entity. All the rest has come from that. The hostility between the two is thus recent and entirely open to analysis.

A program for creating a Greater Serbia at the expense

---

*There is no ethnic distinction among Serbs, Croatians, and Bosnian Moslems. They are all the same people speaking the same language, but they have experienced different histories, the Croatians as part of the Catholic Hapsburg system, the Serbs in the Orthodox Byzantine Empire and then under Moslem Ottoman occupation, and the third group those who converted to the Islamic religion, and usually prospered as agents of the occupying power. (The Bosnian Moslems are also held to have accepted this religious conversion because their real belief was the Manichaean or Gnostic Bogomil heresy, ferociously hostile to the Orthodox church. Hence, alliance with the Moslem Ottomans, equally hostile to Orthodoxy, was a prudent step.)

of Croatians and Bosnians was advocated by intellectuals close to the royalist wartime guerrilla leader Dragoljub Mihajlovic, who was abandoned by the Allies during World War II in favor of Tito, and was executed by Tito in 1946. (He said when he was condemned in Belgrade in 1946, "I wanted much. I started much. But the wind that shook the world carried me and my work away.") A similar program was proposed by the scholars of the Serbian Academy of Sciences in the 1980s, after the death of Tito, and this served as one justification for the war of national expansion which the Serbian government of Slobodan Miloscvic undertook against Slovenia, Croatia, and Bosnia-Herzegovina in 1991, when these others, despite their minority populations of Serbs, declared their national independence.

The war was produced by the determination of the Slovenians, the Croatians, and the dominant communities of Bosnia-Herzegovina to make each of their nations sovereign, and the equal determination of the Serbs that they should not do so on terms that incorporated their Serbian minority populations. The establishment of Serbia, Croatia, and Slovenia as ethnic nations produced the destruction of the community which wished not to be such, the one which identified itself as Bosnian—a geographical designation, not an ethnic one. "Bosnian" also became, after the invasion of Bosnia-Herzegovina, a political identification as well, that of a commitment to secular and non-ethnic politics in what had been Yugoslavia—hence a commitment to a liberal future.

Nationalism is most ferocious when it is frustrated, as it had been in the old Yugoslav federation. The troubles caused throughout the Balkans and Southeastern Europe at the beginning of the 1990s, as in the states issued from the Soviet

200 Union, have not resulted from external threats but from the anxieties caused by the existence of national or ethnic minorities in countries where other communities are dominant. In each of these countries, the minority is perceived as a threat to the integrity of the host nation, producing a hostility which reinforces the insecurity of the minority. Because the minority is where it is, it causes the government under which its members live (and the majority population as well) to believe that it is naturally subversive of the majority order, and represents an actual or potential irredentism on the part of the country where its nationality is the majority. The concern of that country's government and public for the minorities outside its frontiers is taken as proof of this. The prime minister of Hungary in 1992, Jozsef Antall, declared that he was the prime minister of 15 million Hungarians. As there are only 10.4 million Hungarians inside Hungary, his claim naturally lent authority to the charge that Hungarians who are citizens of other countries are future if not present subversives, potential agents of Hungarian national expansion.

In Central and Balkan Europe all sides are victims of the historical admixture of nationalities in the former Ottoman and Hapsburg regions caused by the pattern of successive population migrations. (The situation in the former U.S.S.R. results from that too, but also from a cynical Stalinist policy of displacing nationalities in order to create nationality conflicts where they had not previously existed, in order to divide opposition to his rule.) While the Hapsburg and Ottoman systems survived, the authorities dealt with their subjects in terms of their religious or social identities and communities, in their layered existence, so to speak, usually without recognizing vertical separations between them. When a modern state structure was imposed upon this complexity the pro-crustean result was that described in Chapters 4 and 5. The state never fully coincided with the national group, and some groups—Jews, Gypsies, the different Christian groups as such—had no state at all. The result generally was worsened relations among these groups when they became nations, or national minorities in other nations, putting pressure on new frontiers that had no "natural" basis but were the result of past dynastic divisions or wars, or were the well-intentioned work of the staffs of the Quai d'Orsay and the Foreign Office, or of Walter Lippmann and his colleagues in Washington in 1917–1918. The Transylvanian Hungarians were a power to themselves in the Middle Ages, were autonomous in the seventeenth century, and belonged to Austria in the eighteenth century, to Hungary after 1848, to Romania after 1918, to Hungary again in 1940, and again to Romania from the end of the Second World War to the present day. (The 1989 revolution overthrowing the Ceausescus began in Transylvania.) And Transylvania's is a simple case.

The most acute contemporary problems of nationalism exist in these regions, since these states are reasonably well armed (in the ex–Soviet Union, some still with nuclear weapons) and given to the aggressive affirmation of what in fact are insecure national identities. They demonstrated this before 1918 and in the run-up to the Second World War, and they have done so again since 1989. Balkan war is a process in contemporary history, not a simple series of events.

Nationalism's rival, internationalism, has had three important modern secular manifestations. The first was Marxism, given political existence in the three Socialist Internationals and the Communist system established after 1945. The sec-

202   ond was Nazi racialism, which attempted to impose the rule
       of the Nordic peoples on allegedly lesser races, peoples, and
       their nations. The third is liberal internationalism.

       One must acknowledge that racism without Nazism is
       an international phenomenon too, but not an international-
       ist one. When it takes political form it is as nationalism.
       Anti-Semitism is a peculiarly pervasive international phe-
       nomenon, not only because of the Christian doctrinal claim
       to have superseded Judaism, with consequent traditional
       hostility in the Christian countries to Jews and Judaism, but
       also because anti-Semitism is often linked to class hostilities,
       and is a convenient vehicle for the popular disposition to seek
       conspiratorial explanations for political events. (Hence the
       strange affair, mentioned earlier, of Japanese anti-Semitism.)
       Anti-Semitism's political expression, like that of racism, or-
       dinarily takes nationalistic form, although an anti-Zionism
       for practical purposes indistinguishable from anti-Semitism
       is a political cause in most of the Islamic world.

       Liberal internationalism, like nationalism, is a phenom-
       enon of the nineteenth and twentieth centuries. It proposes a
       modern political replacement for the cultural international-
       ism lost with nationalism's rise.* The dynastic international
       system restored after the Napoleonic wars by the Congress

---

*The Catholic school before Vatican II was probably the last popular
agency of internationalist consciousness in the modern West. It instructed
its pupils that they were not only citizens of their country but members of
a global, Latin-speaking institution, with fellow members and fellow
thinkers everywhere. The novelist and essayist Mary McCarthy writes of
another of its advantages: "To care for the quarrels of the past, to identify
oneself with a cause that became, politically speaking, a losing cause with
the birth of the modern world, is to experience a kind of straining against
reality, a rebellious non-conformity that, again, is rare in America, where
children are instructed in the virtues of the system they live under, as
though history had achieved a happy ending in American civics."

of Vienna began to come apart again with the revolutions of   *203*
1848 and the mounting influence of republican and nationalist sentiments in Europe. In these circumstances, a reform of
international relations on the basis of an extended system of
international law seemed a natural progression, one which
already had taken place inside modern states, where justice
had been depersonalized and legal rights based on equity and
citizenship been substituted for the claims of blood and status. Commerce equally had moved to the impersonal relationships of contract, of anonymous vendor and purchaser.

A theory of international law had existed since the seventeenth century, in the writings of Hugo Grotius, although
Hobbes and others subsequently denied the possibility of
true international law, since no international authority existed to enforce it. Nonetheless, the treaties made between
states, and an increasing number of international agreements
among the major powers dealing with problems of commerce, navigation, piracy, neutrality and blockade, and so
on, were in the nineteenth century generally observed as if
they were law, and these constituted a core of international
legality which was rapidly added to in the later nineteenth
century. The Geneva Convention of 1864 dealt with humane
treatment of the wounded in war. Conventions were agreed
to on the status of prisoners of war, and on international
communications, salvage, the suppression of international
trade in prostitution, the regulation of transportation and
posts, and other matters.

The Hague conferences of 1899 and 1907 attempted to
reduce the level of national armaments and established a
number of agreements concerning the conduct of war. The
Hague Tribunal was established in 1899 as a permanent court

204   of arbitration among nations. In 1910 Andrew Carnegie, the steel magnate—a Scottish optimist—founded his Endowment for International Peace, giving the instruction that "[w]hen . . . war is discarded as disgraceful to civilized man, the Trustees will please then consider what is the next most degrading evil or evils whose banishment . . . would most advance the progress, elevation and happiness of man. . . ."

From this background came three major twentieth-century attempts to make a fundamental reform in international relationships, two of them universal, one regional. These are the League of Nations, the United Nations, and the European Community. The League of Nations, whatever its merits, was undermined by the rise of Fascist dictatorships and aggression, and collapsed at the onset of the Second World War.

The United Nations organization was formed by the victorious Allied powers after the Second World War, and has since done much useful work in technical and humanitarian matters, but until the late 1980s it was paralyzed in major political disputes by the cold war and the great-power veto. It has since gained new support as an agency of international consensus in attempting to mediate conflicts, in peacekeeping, and (in the Kuwait case) for redressing aggression. However, it bears little resemblance to that "Parliament of man, the Federation of the world," to which its founders, like Tennyson, aspired: when "the war-drum throbb'd no longer, and the battle-flags were furl'd." It functions only when the major powers represented on the Security Council want it to function. None have yielded any measure of sovereignty to it, and none presently intends to do so.

The ambition to create a "new world order," proclaimed

by the American government at the time of the Gulf War, and presumably implying a new authority for the UN, was a sketchy conception and on the evidence not a serious one. Mr. Bush's proposal was in the direct line of a twentieth-century American reformist internationalism which assumes that an assembly of governments provides, at least potentially, a form of world democracy. The vast majority of the UN's members are actually unrepresentative governments, class- or interest-bound oligarchies or dictatorships, or outright despotisms. Of the UN's Security Council, one of the five permanent members is a single-party dictatorship with an abominable record of human rights abuse, and a second was such until very recently. It seems scarcely the agency for establishing world democracy and international respect for human rights. But then one must doubt that world democracy or international respect for human rights will be established.

The European Community is the most complex, interesting, realistic, and successful modern effort to establish an international system in which there is a cession of sovereignty to a supranational authority. The Community began with Jean Monnet's proposal to the French government in 1949 that France place its coal and steel industries, which were at the time its essential warmaking capacities, under a common authority with those of Germany. This offer was formally made to Germany on the ninth of May, 1950, was joined by the Benelux countries and Italy, and resulted in the Treaty of Paris of 1951, the document from which the European Community has come. It was a practical economic and technical agreement devoted to a high political purpose, the intermingling of European warmaking resources in order to make another war among the West European powers impossible.

•

The Community exists because of the two European civil wars. Their outcome left Europe broken in power, with the Soviet Union and the United States dominating its two halves. This was a fundamental change in the distribution and dimensions of global power, producing a great change in the perceptions of Europeans. Before, Europe was itself the arena of determinant international action and national rivalries, dominating not only the European stage but world affairs. When the catastrophe was finally over in 1945, the Western Europeans were compelled to reexamine what they were and what they might become. The creation of "Europe" followed from their recognition that without reconciliation their moral survival was in doubt. As Konrad Adenauer, West Germany's postwar chancellor, said to Jean Monnet, when the Frenchman conveyed to him the French government's proposal for the coal and steel community: "For me, like you, this project is of the highest importance: it is a matter of morality. We have a moral and not just a technical responsibility to our people, and that makes it incumbent upon us to fulfill this great hope. . . . I have waited twenty-five years for a move like this. . . . Germany knows that its fate is bound up with that of Western Europe as a whole."

Monnet's genius was to pursue political objectives by means of practical steps in economic and industrial cooperation, of self-evident utility. "Europe" was not to be made according to an overall design, but by beginning at the beginning: through cooperation on tangible and useful projects of common advantage. This method was followed in the Treaty of Rome in 1957, which created the European Economic Community, and the White Paper of 1985 which set the goal of creating a Single European Market by 1993. This

plan was put forward at a moment when momentum had
been lost in the Community's economic as well as its political
integration. By setting a schedule for meeting the new objectives, and proposing reviews of progress at the end of each
six-month term of national presidency of the Community,
the authors of the plan galvanized not only governments and
politicians but the business and industrial communities
whose fortunes would be advanced by the success of a truly
pan-European marketplace.

It was understood that political consequences would follow from this ambitious program to eliminate all barriers to
trade and movement among the twelve members of the community, and to harmonize their fiscal and banking systems.
The president of the European Commission, Jacques Delors,
subsequently said that political union was "the ultimate objective of the Single European Act." But the actual attempt to
move from an integrated economic union to a political union
possessing federal powers, including the power to conduct a
common foreign and security policy for Europe, was made
only in the Maastricht Treaty proposal, put before the European governments at the end of 1991. The governments
agreed to this ambitious political program, but had then to
consult parliaments or public for its ratification, and there
they encountered difficulties, which were, fundamentally,
those posed by nationalism among the European peoples—
their reluctance to yield national political sovereignty.

Acknowledgment of a common European interest and
moral purpose had not extinguished the divergent and sometimes conflicting practical interests and perceptions of the
European states. It was possible, although difficult, to accommodate these within the European Community between

208   1951 and 1993 precisely because Europe remained far from
political integration. France and Germany themselves, and
the two with Italy and the three Benelux countries—the
founding Six—found much common agreement because they
were mutually dependent and culturally close. The three
principal countries were, when the Community began, governed by Christian Democrats, or coalitions in which Christian Democratic parties were dominant, and the Social
Democratic movements which subsequently came to power
(Socialist in France, but rapidly becoming Social Democratic) had, or soon acquired, equally wide agreement on what
Western Europe could and should become.

Postwar Germany needed to be readmitted to the society of the European democracies and to gain economic access to the resources and markets of its neighbors. Italy was
in roughly the same situation. France, humiliated in the war
even if a nominal victor, needed an alliance of the Europeans,
in which it played the principal part, in order to reestablish a
European great-power role the French wanted not only for
France's sake but for that of Europe itself, otherwise seem-
ingly fated to permanent domination by the United States or
the Soviet Union—or by the two together, in an unavowed,
or even unrecognized, but mutually reinforcing collaboration. The Europe of the Six was a club of the war's losers—
the occupied and the defeated of both sides. Just for that
reason it was free to construct "Europe." There was little to
lose and much to gain, and, in the event, the affair was a great
success.

Britain's historical experience with the European continent, and in particular with its ancient rival France, as well as
its twentieth-century enemy Germany, initially caused it to

refuse a European integration in which these countries would be its equals. General de Gaulle's veto in 1963 of the application Britain finally did make to join the Community merely ratified the decision Britain itself had taken in 1945— correctly, in the general's view. When Britain eventually did join—was compelled to do so by the bleakness of the alternative—together with two other peripheral Atlantic states, Denmark and Ireland, the area of common political agreement was reduced, as it was when Greece was invited to join, in 1981, out of Western Europe's concern to reinforce democracy in that country after the interlude of the generals' dictatorship. In 1986, released from the dictatorships of Francisco Franco and Antonio de Oliveira Salazar, Spain and Portugal also became members of the Community.

The liberation of Eastern and Central Europe in 1989 then provided further complication to the effort to redefine the political identity of the new Europe. What now is the Czech Republic, Poland, and Hungary are states essential to the European historical identity. However, they are not West European states, and the Community is West European. They are Central European states, and in 1989 Germany too became a Central European state—once again. Its capital again became Berlin, a city farther to the east than Plzeň in Czechoslovakia. The Germany of Konrad Adenauer, a founder of the European Community, was Rhineland Germany, Catholic and western-looking. Adenauer greatly distrusted the middle-European Germany of shifting eastern frontiers and sense of mission to the backward and pagan East.

Bulgaria, Romania, Serbia—and Greece—are on the other side of the great schism which divided Christianity in the early Middle Ages, and for long periods they were also

210   under Moslem rule. Then there is Moslem Europe itself: the former Bosnia-Herzegovina, nearly 40 percent Moslem at the time war began there; Kosovo and Sanjak in the new Serbian-Macedonian federation, ethnically Albanian, and Albania itself, all of them largely Moslem; and Turkey, partly in Europe and partly in Asia, but a candidate for membership in the European Community.

Two fundamental and related divisions in public opinion and policy choice emerged in the Community as a result of the events of the late 1980s. The first choice concerned admission of the East and Central European states, and is usually described as that between a "widened" Europe rapidly extended eastwards and a Europe "deepened" by means of the closer political and economic integration of the states that are already members of the Community (together with the West European and Scandinavian candidates for immediate membership). Both are held possible in principle, but in practice one has tended to exclude the other. The formulas offered to reconcile the differences include making the Community one of "variable geometry" or with several classes of membership, or developing a European "space" or commonwealth in parallel with the Community. The political form of Europe in the future has variously been described as a tree of branches growing from a strong trunk, or as a Greek temple, its pediment supported by the separate pillars of foreign and defense policy unity, economic integration, and internal security collaboration, each representing a distinct and different cession of national sovereignty by the member states. However, it is difficult to see how either vision can be reconciled with that fully integrated and politically united Europe proposed in the Maastricht Treaty.

Thus, disagreement existed in the early 1990s between those inside the existing Community who may be called federalists, who from the beginning have believed in the possibility of uniting Europe under a single political authority in a manner resembling the union of the United States in the eighteenth century, and those others, like the British and Danes, who want a looser political association. They, together with the Netherlands, Ireland, and Portugal, have also wanted a Community closely linked to the United States as a counterweight to the big European states. The identity and autonomy of the small nations, and sometimes their national existence itself, has always had to be defended against self-aggrandizing neighbors. Inside the Community this problem still exists, if in undramatic form. It is the fundamental problem of small states adjacent to big ones. Historically, the small states have constantly looked for external support for their political independence and cultural autonomy: Ireland from France; the Belgians and Portuguese from Britain; the Danes through solidarity with the other Scandinavians, and in particular by means of the Scandinavian neutrality which Hitler breached in 1940 by invading Denmark and Norway. An open and inclusive Europe, with as many members as possible, with close ties to the United States, and with the influence of Germany and France reduced, would almost automatically be a confederal Europe, rather than the political union the Twelve said they wanted when they negotiated the Maastricht Treaty.

A confederal Europe would have no common foreign policy, or at least an extremely restricted one, the good intentions of the Maastricht signatories notwithstanding. To find a common external policy of any consequence for a Europe in-

212   corporating Germany, France, Britain, Denmark, Greece, the Low Countries, Spain, Portugal, and Italy, plus neutral Ireland and Sweden, and Austria, and perhaps the Czech Republic and Slovakia, Poland, Hungary, Romania, Bulgaria, the Baltic states, and possibly Malta and Cyprus as well, is clearly impossible. Britain, France, the Netherlands, Portugal, Spain, and even Denmark all are former imperial powers, with histories of exploration and conquest, domination of the Americas, the Indies and Africa, and populating new nations in the Americas and Oceania. They do not have the political habits and reactions appropriate to members of a federation. They expect to have an independent say in international affairs. Britain may act in concert with the United States, but when Mrs. Thatcher was its prime minister she certainly considered herself to be working with—and at times working through—Presidents Reagan and Bush. She was not their lieutenant but their ally. France notoriously expects to be heard on world affairs, and to act independently in response to world problems. This increasingly is true of Spain, in the seventeenth century the greatest European power.

There are other important divisions in Europe. Britain still has Commonwealth connections with India, the Caribbean, Africa, Canada, Australia, and New Zealand. Spain regards itself as having a special relationship with the Islamic world, of which it was once a part, as well as with Latin America. France and Italy, former colonial powers in Africa, also claim distinct roles and responsibilities in the region, and a special vulnerability as well, since, with Spain and Portugal, they are the main objects of African and North African immigration, both legal and clandestine. France historically has been the protector of the Christians of Lebanon. Germany was for many years an ally of Turkey.

These relationships in one respect may be assets for Eu- rope, but they are also obstacles to the development of a common policy even on the relatively straightforward issues of the Middle East and Persian Gulf. They were responsible for the Community's catastrophic failure to find a united response of any weight to aggression, war, and ethnic purge in Yugoslavia in 1991–1993—a challenge to the fundamental ambition and achievement of the West Europeans, which has been Western Europe's pacification, an accomplishment that had seemed to demonstrate that liberal internationalism could, after all, provide a valid response to the historical problem of national aggrandizement and international violence. The failure to meet the Yugoslav test was an event of the greatest importance, to which I will return.

There is another successful case of liberal internationalism today, whose existence tends often to be overlooked. This is the immense, complex, yet informal web of practical associations which has developed among the contemporary democracies. Largely since the Second World War, the western democracies have created a very extensive network of cooperative institutions and associations, beginning with the UN itself and its specialized agencies, including the World Bank, the International Monetary Fund, and General Agreement on Tariffs and Trade. All are the product of decisions taken by Franklin Roosevelt and Winston Churchill at the Atlantic Conference of 1941.

There are the Council of Europe, the Organization for Economic Cooperation and Development (which originated as the agency directing the use of Marshall Plan aid), the European Community itself, the European Free Trade Association, the European Bank for Reconstruction and

214   Development, the Group of Seven finance ministers' meetings and the annual economic "summits," NATO, the North Atlantic Council, the Western European Union, the Conference on Security and Cooperation in Europe, and so on. In addition, there are thousands, possibly hundreds of thousands, of semi-public or private institutions of cooperation acting across the frontiers of the democracies and beyond them, from multinational corporations to academic seminars and journals, some self-interested, some devoted to the public interest, but all together providing a dialogue of unprecedented intensity, complexity, and breadth.

This amounts to an unacknowledged commonwealth of the democratic states, and is the second of the crucial achievement of the postwar years. It is often taken for granted, or even ignored, by those looking for more glamorous forms of institutionalized world order. However, it is neglected to our risk, since it is possible for this intense yet utterly realistic form of international cooperation based on shared values to falter—as indeed, in the early 1990s, began to happen with respect to international economic and trade relations.

In the years leading up to 1989 it was the magnetism of the democracies' cooperative successes which irresistibly drew Eastern Europe and the Soviet Union towards western political values. Afterwards, a still higher level of effective international cooperation was expected, probably institutionalized under the United Nations. The successful mobilization of a UN coalition to fight the Gulf War in 1991 reinforced that expectation. Then came 1992, a year of European deconstruction, and of a new and devastating European war in the Balkans. A political crisis resulted from the controversy over further European political unification, gener-

ated by popular opposition to the cessions of sovereignty **215**
embodied in the Maastricht Treaty. The war in what had
been Yugoslavia, and the failure of the liberal democracies to
do anything serious to halt it, dealt a brutal blow to the idea
that the democracies possessed the capacity, or the will, to
enlarge that zone of pacification and cooperation created inside the western political community. It even raised a question as to the whether that achievement itself would last. Was
Western Europe enduringly united? Was Atlantic cooperation permanently installed? For the first time since the Second World War it became possible to doubt the answers to
those questions. It was possible to see 1992–1993 as having
terminated the postwar world. It was possible to interpret the
Yugoslav War as a blow to liberal internationalism equivalent
to the failure of the League of Nations in the 1930s to deal
with Fascist and Nazi aggression.

The European Community's own development had run
into the contradiction in its own ambition, to create a
"union" of "sovereign" states. Europe actually had to be one
or the other. The public in the member states proved reluctant to make more than a limited grant of political and security sovereignty to the supranational institutions of the
European Community, even though they thoroughly ap-
proved of "Europe." The European governments were
blocked from finding a common policy even on so urgent a
matter as the war in Yugoslavia not only because of the mediocrity of western Europe's leadership in 1991–1992 (and that
of the United States) but because of the peoples' divergent
sense of their national interests and the influence of their individual national historical experiences and conditioning—
the separate experiences of these distinct peoples with

216   respect to war and foreign intervention—which led each of them in a different direction.

Even before the Yugoslav crisis, the West Europeans had been unable to agree on an active common policy towards Palestinians and Israel. They disagreed over the Suez intervention, the Vietnam War, and the Falklands reconquest. They could not agree on naval intervention in the Persian Gulf during the Iran-Iraq War: some took part, some did not. Some joined the UN coalition which waged war against Iraq in 1991, and some disapproved.

The Community has failed for years now to agree on what to do about membership for the former Communist states, producing only temporizing political and economic measures, while West European lobbies blocked the opening of European markets to the farm produce and low-technology manufactured goods in which East European producers have a comparative advantage. The West Europeans failed to do much that was serious to reinforce the security of the eastern countries, despite the latter's anxious demands and new fears in the aftermath of the sterile certainties of the cold war. This might have been done through NATO; or through the Western European Union, the Europeans' own security organization, which predates NATO; or with new politico-military measures. There were no effective steps to mediate, moderate, or deflect the consequences of conflicting ethnic claims and interests in ex-Communist Europe, despite the West's own fundamental interest in trans-European stability and order.

The Community's failure with respect to ex-Yugoslavia was not for lack of mechanisms for policy agreement, as some have argued, since communications among Europe's

foreign offices and embassies remained in perfect order. The   *217*
proposed Maastricht arrangements for establishing a common European foreign and security policy would simply
have worsened the situation by confirming the principle of
unanimity on major decisions, thus institutionalizing stale-
mate. There was never, in the course of the Yugoslav crisis,
any formal obstacle to Paris's—or London's, or even The
Hague's—taking matters into national hands and recruiting
a coalition that agreed on a particular policy, as the United
States had done the year before with respect to Kuwait and
Iraq. The challenge was not to send a huge army to pacify
Yugoslavia and impose an externally determined political order upon an insurgent population, as some in western governments and the press made out. It was to intervene first of
all politically to require strict and internationally supervised
guarantees of minority rights in the new states being granted
recognition. Second, it was to punish acts of aggression
when they were first committed, and invasions, overt or
covert, across recognized frontiers. It was third to halt and
punish, when they were first discovered, those crimes
against international law and humanity which had not been
committed in Europe since 1945: systematic attacks on civil-
ian populations; terrorization of civilians for the purpose of
ethnic "cleansing"; the employment of rape as an instrument
of terrorization and ethnic purge; the razing of towns; the
destruction of churches, mosques, libraries, and historical
monuments—places of peoples' civilization and collective
memory; the beginnings of extermination in internment
camps, all of this attested to in the reports on human rights
abuse compiled by former Polish prime minister Tadeusz
Mazowiecki at international request, which found no practical sequel. None of the European governments had the

218 stomach to act on any of this, nor did the American.

Governments in the twelve Community countries saw the Yugoslav problem in different ways, and were therefore unable to act collectively, and refused to act individually. None even considered assuming individual national leadership. In this respect France bears the principal blame, since it was the one major European power in a position to act in Yugoslavia (with Germany precluded from doing so by its wartime record in the Balkans and the British government obsessed with the Ulster precedent). It is also the one which has constantly demanded in the past that Europe take responsibility for its independent interests when these are threatened. In the event, France and the other West European powers demonstrated that they could not or would not defend the new standards of interstate conduct, legality, and political morality established in Western Europe after the Second World War. The United States did so as well, of course; but this was above all a European problem.

The Yugoslav War was a crucial blow to the ideals, and what had been the accomplishments, of liberal internationalism, because aggression and ethnic purge in the former Yugoslavia amounted to a deliberate and successful defiance of what had been thought a new European and international order. The European Community, the international community as organized in the United Nations, and the individual western powers all failed to anticipate, prevent, reverse, or impose effective sanctions in response to the war and the crimes which were part of it.

The existence of the European Community and of the United Nations actually proved an obstacle to action, by in-

hibiting individual national action and rationalizing the refusal to act nationally. The Community and the UN at the
same time proved unable to agree on any joint measures going beyond humanitarian assistance together with ineffectual
negotiations whose eventual, if unmeant, effect was to ratify
aggression and ethnic purge.

Invidious ethnic discrimination followed by aggressive
and expansionist war, ethnically motivated population purges
and transfers generating refugees in the hundreds of thousands, the employment of terror and of rape as instruments of
national expansion, all returned to Europe. The failure of the
European powers, the United States, and the United Nations
to deal with the crisis provided a devastating demonstration
of the limits of contemporary liberal internationalism. It revealed the inability of groups or committees of democratic
governments to employ force and assume risks, or, in the case
of economic sanctions, even to accept serious inconvenience
to one or another of the group, when the danger of non-ac-
tion is not direct and urgent for each.

In the Gulf War a coalition led by the United States had
gone to war, and subsequently had attempted to deprive Iraq
of weapons of mass destruction and to protect the Kurdish
and Shi'ite minorities of that country. This occurred only
because the United States defined the problem and a presumed solution, organized the coalition, and then led it into
action. In the Bosnian crisis, the United States did not act, so
everyone failed to act, or acted only after so many thresholds
of legal transgression and moral outrage had been passed
that it was too late for the principle of collective peacekeeping (or peacemaking) to survive as a plausible guarantee of
international society's security in the future. Aggression was

220   a success. Ethnic purge had been demonstrated an effective instrument of national expansion. Liberal internationalism was defeated. The lesson was not lost on others.

Nor was the failure a single one. The UN's Somalia, Lebanon, Israel, and Cyprus operations had long been matters of frustration. Even the outcome of the Gulf War proved unsatisfactory: Saddam Hussein left triumphantly in power, his conduct and brutal methods of government unchanged by the UN coalition's intervention of 1991, Iraq's Kurdish and Shi'ite minorities still in jeopardy.

The efficacy of UN operations had always depended upon the assumption (or the myth) that a limited deployment of UN soldiers represented the will of an overwhelming part of the international community, hence that the UN forces had to be respected for the practical reason that if they were not, large-scale reinforcement or powerful retaliation would follow. In 1992 the spell of this was broken by the actions of Serbian, Croatian, and Moslem militias in ex-Yugoslavia, by Saddam Hussein's not unsuccessful resistance to UN resolutions and arms inspectors, and by the inability of UN intervention to deal even with the anarchical forces at loose in certain countries in Africa—the one place where UN military action was actually taken. The UN's commitments were not credible because they were not backed up by the national commitment of the countries supplying the forces. Australia's minister of defense said at the moment his troops left for Cambodia in April 1992 that if a single soldier were killed by the Khmer Rouge, all the Australians would be withdrawn. The same, or something close to it, was true for most of the countries furnishing UN troops. A fundamental cause

of the failure to intervene effectively in ex-Yugoslavia was the
western countries' reluctance to place their soldiers at risk in
the abstract interests of liberal internationalist order. (In this
respect France was exemplary: it had the largest UN contin-
gent in Yugoslavia and accepted by far the largest number of
casualties there.)

The progress made by liberal internationalism during
the postwar half century has been the product of forces that
are waning and conditions that have ceased to exist. In Europe this progress rested on the desire of the West Europeans to create a new relationship among themselves, which
in essential respects they have done. They have created what
Charles de Gaulle called a *Europe des patries*, an expression
signifying much more than a "Europe of nations." It means a
Europe of homelands—fatherlands. It is a radical conception, not in the least like that of the American federal union,
which associated individual colonial settlements possessing a
common language, history, literature, and political culture.
The European union was meant as a triumph of common
civilization over particular histories.

This European achievement was undermined in 1992–
1993 by the attempt to go beyond it. This occurred because
the power of nationalism was not respected: the force of the
individual's attachment to his *patrie*. The West Europeans
founded their Community because the world wars had devastated them and the cold war posed not only a military and
political danger but a moral threat to European civilization.
They also benefited from the presence of a benevolent and
essentially disinterested American protecting power. Obviously the strategic interests of the United States were served

222   by Europe's security, and Americans saw the unification of Europe as serving this purpose. But Americans also wanted Europe's unification as a support to the values and common political standards shared on the two sides of the Atlantic.

When the crisis arrived in Europe in 1992, it was no longer possible for the United States to play the protector's role. Washington no longer was willing to pay the costs of leadership. It did not possess the financial means it had in the past; it had heavily indebted itself, and become dependent upon its creditors. The historical isolationism of the American popular temper returned, reinforced by a sense of victimization in trade matters, at a time of general international economic difficulties. Popular attention and energies were redirected, for good reason, to the domestic economy and domestic social issues.

The country's capacity for global military intervention remained very great; with the collapse of the Soviet Union the United States had no rival in this respect. However, having lost the will independently to finance global intervention, the United States, under the Reagan and Bush administrations, had demanded that other governments finance the deployment of American troops abroad, and even their interventions in Central America. This automatically was a forfeiture of leadership. The American military had also adopted a doctrine of acting only under conditions of overwhelming advantage or virtual invulnerability, and this was put forward as an objection to new foreign interventions. Not only had Vietnam left the American public reluctant to risk casualties in the service of an abstract program of international order (which is what they had believed the United States to be about in Vietnam), but American generals them-

selves had become convinced that they must never again be-   *223*
gin any action in which they might fail.

The West Europeans' intention in building the Community was to reestablish on modern terms the internationalism and pan-European consciousness that had characterized Europe from the time of Charlemagne to the eighteenth century.* The spirit of the Community was to be that of a willing subordination of nation to civilization, in a system in which each national personality, and the particular interests of each historical nation, could be accommodated in a new manner which transcended the nations. There were to be functional levels at which sovereignty would reside, according to the scale of the problem and of the appropriate response. The enterprise was practical at the same time that it was visionary.

Its setbacks during 1992 and 1993 were not fatal. But they made it plain that the Europeans had to return to the sources of their "Europe," which were the visionary pragmatism of Monnet and his colleagues, and de Gaulle's recognition of the primordial importance of nation to any European internationalism—this "ensemble of indestructible nations, forged by the fire of history, each having its face, its character, its traditions, often opposed to one an-

---

*A British reviewer, Oswyn Murray, wrote in the *Times Literary Supplement* in August 1991, "There was once a culture which embraced all of Europe, indeed all of recorded time, and which included in its sphere all the sciences known to man. From the fifteenth to the eighteenth centuries, natural scientist could dispute with theologian, astronomer with philologist, philosopher with antiquary, from Prague and Buda to Leipzig and Leiden, across frontiers of religion and of race, in a tongue which all could understand—Latin, the universal language of science. Then it was possible to discuss Spinoza alongside Lucretius, to match Vida with Virgil, to compare Descartes and Bacon with Plato and Aristotle, to find Kepler writing a Pindaric ode and Bentley lecturing on Newton."

224   other by terrible griefs, and centuries of battle, which can and must reunite . . ."

Americans and Europeans wanted to see the eruption of Balkan violence in 1992–1993 not as a contradiction of Europe's progress and new order but as the last convulsion of an old and primitive Europe. What it actually demonstrated was that the European postwar evolution was fragile, and that confronted with the malign power of nationalist violence and passion, liberal internationalism would yield.

The collapse of Communism, the peace which has in general prevailed since 1945, and the very high material standard of life achieved by the liberal democracies, with all of their very complex and creative forms of cooperative action and mutual understanding, have combined to make it possible in recent years to believe that the horrors—indeed "history"—are behind us. The Yugoslav War has demonstrated that this is not true.

There has, moreover, been a fundamental change in Europe's geopolitical situation. The two powers which since 1918 dominated events in Central and Eastern Europe are now destabilized, Russia obviously so, grievously weakened by its economic collapse and political revolution. It remains a country of immense resources and a profound national consciousness, the latter linked to its historical sense of itself as "the Third Rome," its destiny held to be to redeem mankind from the predicament and tragedy of history. Both Bolshevik empire (and mission) and czarist empire now have been lost. The Russian people have been humiliated. They now are surrounded by societies of even greater weakness, experiencing violence linked to their own unfulfilled nationalisms and ethnic hatreds. Germany, stable for forty-four years within the

partition imposed by defeat, now is reestablished in frontiers
which some still contest. It has lost the social consensus that
prevailed in western Germany during those four decades, and
the social discipline Communism enforced in the East. Its anchorage in the European Community has been loosened by
the Community's institutional crisis and the drift of the
United States away from European commitments.

Central and Eastern Europe and the Balkans have in the
past been the dependents, and victims, of Russia and Germany. The issue now to be settled is what will happen in, or
to, the independence which these nations recaptured in 1989,
an independence that was never solid before, and which now
invokes myths of antique nationhood, sovereignties ex-
punged, the legacy of the crimes and glories of the past, at a
moment when the political and economic realities of these
states impose great hardships. Theirs is a slender and recent
independence, a late turn in a history characterized by domination, submission, and much suffering. Their situation is
quite as explosive as it was during the first two decades of this
century. The 1918 settlements provided no solution, only
complication. Since 1989 dreadfully little has been done to
give the new governments and the economies of the region
anchorage in pan-European and larger international structures, or to assure their security within their present borders
against the threats to one another inherent in their national
and ethnic claims and divisions.* There has been no serious
attempt by the democracies to establish a system for the arbitration and negotiation of minority conflict and frontier
challenges among these troubled states.

*See the present writer's "Invitation to War," *Foreign Affairs*, New York,
Summer 1993.

226   The gravity of the situation which results remains poorly appreciated. Once again Europe has shown its vulnerability when faced with the old furies of ideological extravagance and nihilistic violence which came so close to destroying it before. The Yugoslav War evoked once again the capacity for political crime which has been only provisionally resolved in European civilization since World War II—the capacity for crime, or rather for what Margaret Thatcher, with characteristic bluntness, at the time of the slaughter of Moslem refugees in the town of Srebrenica in April 1993, identified as evil. That word does not ordinarily figure in the vocabulary in which world affairs are discussed.

One has seen in Yugoslavia something which can be called totalitarian nationalism, a modern amalgam of nationalist emotion and apocalyptic expectation, making use of advanced means of communication and propaganda. The same thing gives some sign of developing elsewhere among the shocked and fragmented societies of the ex-Soviet world, as well as in places in the non-western world. The ruthless imposition and then the failure of the Marxist system in the one place, and the effects of colonialism and junk westernization in the other, have left something like an ethical void. The contemporary West has had little to offer in remedy, being itself in very considerable moral confusion. Outside Europe, the anarchy of Somalia and Liberia in the 1990s may prove a paradigm for a good many other societies which have also undergone destructive attack upon their systems of value and their assumptions about the meaning of existence.

Resistance to Communism during the cold war years in most of Eastern Europe found political expressions of a remarkable ethical purity, but for comprehensible and even in-

evitable reasons these have proven difficult to perpetuate in
the troubled circumstances that have followed Communism's
collapse. The liberal and democratic political forces which
have developed there remain extremely important. But the
economic destruction caused by Communism, and the immense difficulties, poverty, and social dislocation involved in
the effort to install a market economy—often maladroitly,
and badly advised (by ideologically committed western coun-
selors)—have contributed to literal demoralization, inviting
the absolutist response. The Polish writer and former dissident Adam Michnik has remarked that "the supreme stage of
Communism is nationalism," in which nationalism discards
the Marxism but maintains its apparatus of social control.
This certainly has been the case in Serbia. A new synthesis of
nationalism with state totalitarianism has been made which
could prove of potent consequences. It is a new force for
mass social mobilization.

There has been much complacence about the outlook
for liberal democracy, particularly in the United States,
where there has never been a real temptation to nihilism
(even if nihilism has now become the practical philosophy of
the urban ghetto). There has never been collective despair,
however isolate and desperate the individual American life.
In Europe the moral possibilities are more complex. Transcendence and nihilism both are always potentially on the
program. There is a capacity to follow a bad idea to its very
end, which the pragmatic tradition—and anti-intellectual-
ism have spared the Anglo-American. There is no political
sentimentality. Europeans have always reproached Americans for sentimentality. Europeans, in their political history,
have lacked the space for sentiment. Others have cause to

228   fear Europeans for this lack of sentimentality.

However, reproaches cannot be limited to Europe. Recent events have again demonstrated a general incapacity of governments responsible to public opinion to deal with problems whose consequences lie in the future. There has been little willingness in the western countries as a whole to enforce an elevated standard of international conduct when the perception of immediate political cost or risk has outweighed the perceived longer-term gain. There is nothing new in this. It has repeatedly been demonstrated in the past that governments passively dependent upon public opinion, as democracies are as a general rule (and properly so), are usually incapable of dealing with long-term threats requiring the serious risk of lost lives and material costs, even when a reasoned case can be made that action in the short term will defend interests and values of the greatest consequence for the future. In the 1930s there was no popular clamor in Britain and France—nor certainly in the United States—for military action to block Hitler's remilitarization of the Rhineland, annexing of Austria, or partition of Czechoslovakia. Chamberlain and Daladier were the popular politicians, considered by the democratic public to be calm and reasonable men, rightly refusing to run risks in order to address merely hypothetical dangers. The public turned to the prophetic but "irresponsible" Churchill and de Gaulle only after all the combinations of appeasement (and collaboration) had been tried and had failed. Those governments which can mobilize their peoples to resolute sacrifice for distant and future causes are the ones led by the Hitlers, Milosevics, and Saddam Husseins. They exploit the real grievances of their peoples and invoke the great myths of national destiny and national persecution in order to win vast sacrifices for an allegedly glorious future. They are never stronger than when they defy the international community and succeed.

There are certain complacencies by which the democracies justify their aversion to sacrifice. These claim that incompetent as the democracies may seem, democracy still is a better system than all the rest, and because they are virtuous, it is said, the democracies will always prevail in the end. Democracies are said never to go to war with democracies, and the world is becoming more democratic. The people are said always to know best. But the fact that democracies do not like sacrifices, do not listen to bad news nor wish to think about bad possibilities in the future, do not want their comfort or profits interfered with, should be accepted with apprehension, not complacence. Why is it evident that democracy and liberal values will prevail? The evidence is very limited, the historical experience with modern democracy brief, of little more than two centuries. We do not know the future of democracy.

In Yugoslavia in 1992 and 1993, those who traveled the war zones could recognize what faction controlled the region by whether it was the mosque, the Catholic church, or the Orthodox church which had been destroyed—sometimes in places which had experienced no other destruction. War in Yugoslavia has incorporated the attempt to desecrate or eradicate values. This was the rationale for the systematic rape of Moslem women: doing so desecrated and "ruined" them. The moral cost paid by the rapist, or the murderer, is recognized, but is assumed. Hamlet's desire was to murder his stepfather in his adultery to be certain that he would go to

230 hell, even though this guaranteed hell for Hamlet as well. The drunkenness of the militias encountered in Yugoslavia is one product of their fearful commitment to an equivalent proposition, and of their rejection of what they had been before, before they had murdered and raped their neighbors, and become changed men. This was in their faces. It was in the urgent lies pressed upon the outsider by the physicians and university professors and other professionals who led the warring factions. They had put aside their laboratory smocks and briefcases and professional consciousnesses to enter a different moral universe of different truth and titanic possibilities—from which one does not return.

The Italian writer Curzio Malaparte, in his hallucinatory account of wartime travels, *Kaputt* (1944), writes of a diplomatic dinner in Helsinki in 1943 at which a guest said of a Russian prisoner of war, a faithful Leninist who had murdered the Lutheran prison pastor whose arguments had shaken his belief in atheism, "He had tried to kill God in the pastor." Another guest, the Turkish ambassador, remarked "The murder of God is in the air; it is an element of modern civilization."

A nineteenth-century English divine and historian, the Bishop of Oxford, William Stubbs, once wrote of the study of history that "though it may make you wise, . . . [it] cannot fail to make you sad." The political defeats liberal internationalism suffered in 1992 and 1993 have a significance which will transcend those years. "Europe's" construction by Monnet, Schuman, De Gasperi, Adenauer, Spaak, de Gaulle, and the others—and by the United States as well, one cannot forget—was the finest achievement of the liberal international-

ist movement of the past century, a symbolic as well as practical repudiation of European civil war. As Monnet said to
Adenauer, it was a moral accomplishment. Its failure as the
1990s began has been a moral debacle. Moral achievements
in history being very rare and precious, such a failure is in
the long run more significant than any strategic or political
defeat.

9 *Progress*

In the First World War a complacent Europe which had too much, was too rich, thought too much, and had invented too much, having created modern civilization and become bored with it, began, in spiritual dissatisfaction and Faustian ambition, to remake itself again, this time through destruction. The undertaking was launched in 1914, culminated in Nazism in the 1940s and in Stalinism between the 1930s and 1950s, and ended, provisionally, in 1989.

The destruction began in an act of Serbian nationalism. It ended in ruins for all of Europe. Germany's conviction that it lacked empire, living space, respect, and national fulfillment led it to national catastrophe in 1918. Britain had defended its national primacy at sea and achieved its aim of keeping continental Europe divided, but the destruction of its world preeminence and empire was begun. France had wanted, and got, Alsace and Lorraine, and revenge, but was physically and morally exhausted as a consequence. Imperial Russia intervened in the war to defend Orthodox Serbia, and ended in an atheist revolution. The Great War was the most important event of the twentieth century.

It was a decisive historical event, a marker. Yet the Second World War was more threatening as an indicator of what might lie in the future. It was a war of ideas—ideas about the future. Since the Enlightenment the West has considered politics a matter of thought; both Nazism and Stalinism were movements of ideas. They were millenarian historical visions which required tens of millions of deaths, a harvest of suffering, ferocious persecutions, expulsions, labor camps, prisons, death camps, the corruption of a generation of thought and language.

Non-ideological politics and war today seem to us retrograde. We have become accustomed to ideology, our own affairs until recently dominated by the ideological cold war and its ancillary events in Asia, the Americas, and the Middle East. We have great difficulty with something like the Yugoslav War because this sort of thing should have been done away with by progress. We see it as an irruption from the past unreasonably imposing itself upon the present.

The politics of ideas produces the cool murderousness of the man of reflection, confident that the harm he does pays the necessary admission to the redeemed Future. Nationalism has about it the sweat of passion and hatred, caused by its belief in the radiant and recuperable past, producing the private readiness to kill neighbor and friend. The Leninist killed for principles; the regrettable deed was done to the thinker's orders by dutiful, or sadistic and therefore irresponsible, executioners. The nationalist has his heart in his work. He is a concrete thinker. He is a limited thinker too, but he acts from the roots of being, of human society, from a given earth and clan—primordial attachments. That is why

234 he causes so much confusion to the man of ideas.

Ideological movements are more dangerous than nationalistic ones because they present abstract solutions of universal application, and because they connect to, and mobilize, permanent elements of irrationality in human conduct: the vulnerability to apocalyptic expectation, the search for temporal salvation, the willingness to believe history a matter of occult and powerful conspiracies, the disposition towards a Manichaean notion of history as the battle between active principles of unnuanced evil and good.

Progressive political thought in the twentieth century, as in the nineteenth, has rested on the assumption that man experiences a natural development towards higher and implicitly more virtuous forms of political and social organization and conduct. The troubled past is interpreted as a product of ignorance, unscientific thought, or superstition, and its manifestations of willful cruelty, greed, and vengeance are assumed to be the product of backwardness.

One might think such figures as Adolf Hitler and Joseph Stalin obstacles to the progressive interpretation of history. Progressive thought ordinarily deals with them by excluding them from the mainstream of history. They are held to be historical outsiders, and their defeat enables progressive history to resume: they are not part of it.

The proposition that such people are contemporary history's insiders, so to speak, not its outsiders—that they are not unrepresentative figures of contemporary history, not isolated and disregardable exceptions—is widely rejected. We see this in the frequent insistence upon separating Stalin, the demonic figure, from Lenin, the supposed progressive one, when considering Soviet history, and in the claim that

Hitler's genocidal attack upon the Jews was a "unique" event, uniquely evil, different from the other racial and social proscriptions and murders of the Nazi regime, or of Stalin's in the U.S.S.R. One has to remark that if the Shoah was indeed unique, there is nothing to learn from it, because by definition it is unrepeatable. I do not think this is so.

There is another view of history, one of a certain pessimism—a tragic pessimism, if you will. It does not and could not deny the obvious development of human institutions toward more and more complex and sophisticated forms: the substitution of contract for blood and kinship obligations, the progress of institutions of justice and the protection of human rights, the extension of democratic political institutions. This view would certainly recognize that the political as well as material conditions of life have grown better for those fortunate enough to live in North America, Western and Central Europe, and a part of Asia. It would also suggest that they have grown markedly worse in much of Africa, another part of Asia, and parts of Latin America, and for specific groups even in the advanced states. It sees that societies progress but also decline: that Europe today is not what it was in the Middle Ages, but that neither is China or the Islamic world, for whom our Middle Ages was a period of prosperity, intellectual and scientific advancement, and stable government—all of which they lack today.

It would observe that history is not a great river, but moves in a multitude of channels at different speeds, and sometimes in different directions. Surely to visit Siena or Florence, or the châteaux of the Loire, is to feel oneself among the monuments of a higher civilization, certainly not a more backward one. A recognition of decline is essential in order to grasp the nature of progress. There has been

236   progress, but the arts and architecture of the high Renaissance, in these examples, are superior to what the late twentieth century offers, and a great many aspects of public life,
public works, and social organization in Renaissance Italy
were also more "progressive" than those of contemporary
Florence or Siena (or New York or London). Something of
the same thing may be said with respect to Greece or the
Rome of the republics—set aside the question of slavery—or
of Han or Tang China.

This view of history says what should be obvious, that
some things get better and some get worse; that moral as well
as institutional progress takes place but also institutional and
moral regression; hence, that the balance of good and evil in
the world—of high-mindedness and low-mindedness—is today much what it was in Neolithic times. The ethnologist
and explorer Michel Peissel has written about a community
of hunters and simple agriculturists he came across in an isolated Himalayan valley, whose customs and beliefs are similar
to what we believe were those of Stone Age Europe—who
would seem essentially unaffected by the outside world since
Neolithic times. They even make rock drawings of ritual significance resembling those found in the caves of southwest-
ern France. His Himalayan people are indistinguishable
from "modern" men in essential conduct and outlook. I myself find this very consoling: the moral constancy and continuity of man through the millennia.

That I am the moral superior of the artist of the Mag-
dalenian caves or of the triumphal way of Persepolis, not to
speak of the tragedian of classical Athens, or that I am more
intelligent or sophisticated than they, seems to me a preposterous and impertinent notion. That my society is more
complex and in important institutional as well as material re-

spects superior to theirs is an acceptable argument, although
one that must be qualified. The liberal West attempts to
practice a disinterested justice and attend impartially to the
needs and interests of its people, and to their freedom; that is
true. But this West also bears responsibility for the ideological totalitarianisms, fixed on terrifying conceptions of virtue
and intolerant universalist visions. The totalitarian ideo-
logues also believed in progressive history possessing meaning and purpose.

The most common form of progressive historical belief
is the simple one that all that has gone on in the past did so in
order to lead up to us, so that we are more advanced, if not
better, than anything before. The meaning of history has
been to produce us, our society—and our future.* However,
the belief that history has a meaning and goal is nothing new;
it has always been the belief of Jews and Christians. Their
conviction, however, is not of human progress. For them,
history is the temporal execution of a plan of God, only im-
perfectly comprehensible by men and women. The responsibility of human beings is to justify themselves. The
fulfillment of history, or its redemption, comes at, and by,
the will of God, not man.

The case we have been considering is that of nationalism
against internationalism. National feelings, profoundly
rooted in the human necessity for identity and connection,
have produced political consequences in our time both sublime and grossly criminal. The reach of nationalism's criminality ordinarily has been limited by the character of

*The Cambridge historian Herbert Butterfield has called this "the Whig
interpretation of history," although it is easily recognized in its natural-
ized American form, that making the United States and American society
is what history has been all about.

238   nationalism itself, whose reference and standard is itself. The affirmation of the nation is an international disturbance to the extent that a nation conceives itself licensed to validate itself by the victimization of another society. But the geographical sweep of this usually is limited. Serbia has wanted to incorporate the lands next to it occupied by other Serbs. Iraq wants Kuwait because it holds that Kuwait's territory belonged to Iraq under the Ottomans and was stolen. Palestinians have wanted what they consider their stolen country. Israelis want a country to survive in. The Vietnamese wanted their own nation.

The person who believes in progress cannot regard the evil in twentieth-century history (the urge to kill God, as Malaparte put it) without either denying part of what is before his eyes or reexamining what he means by progress. We go forward by certain institutional arrangements that ameliorate the way communities deal with one another. We find ways to overcome the limits of our primordial loyalties, or to subsume them into the affirmation of a larger interest, a reconstruction of a political civilization, as the Europeans have specifically tried to do, and as all of the democracies have recently done, in what I have called their inadvertent commonwealth.

But it is a great error to fail to understand the difference between this progress, that of civilization, and the progress of man. The failure to make that distinction gave the world Marxism-Leninism and Nazism, and is perfectly capable of giving us much the same thing again in the future. The crucial truth is that man as such does not grow better. He is free. He remains the beast/angel Pascal called him, a chaos, contradiction, prodigy. He progresses only by recognizing his nature, his misery together with his sublime possibility. A politics has to be built on that.

Works Cited

There follows a list of authors, works, and other sources quoted or directly referred to in the text. As this is a book which falls into the category Trotsky identifies as "the conjectures of dilettantes," a formal apparatus of notes has seemed inappropriate. The quotations which appear in the text illustrate my arguments but do not demonstrate them—I argue about these matters; I cannot prove them, nor can anyone else.

The lines which accompany the dedication are from T. S. Eliot, "East Coker," in *Four Quartets.* New York: Harcourt, Brace, 1943.

Acton, John Emerich Edward Dalberg, Baron, *Essays in the Liberal Interpretation of History.* Chicago: University of Chicago Press, 1967.

——, *Essays on Freedom and Power.* New York: Meridian, 1955.

Adams, Henry, *History of the United States of America During the Administrations of James Madison.* New York: The Library of America, 1986.

——, *History of the United States of America During the Administrations of Thomas Jefferson.* New York: The Library of America, 1986.

Allen, Frederick Lewis, *Only Yesterday.* New York: Bantam, 1959.

Ames, Fisher, quoted in Adams, *History of the United States of America During the Adminstrations of Thomas Jefferson*, q.v.

Anderson, Benedict, *Imagined Communities: Reflections on the Origins and Spread of Nationalism* (revised edition). London: Verso, 1991.

239

240   Angleton, James Jesus, quoted in Mangold, *Cold Warrior*, q. v.

Antall, Jozsef, *The International Herald Tribune*, Paris, January 16, 1993.

Arendt, Hannah, *The Origins of Totalitarianism*. New York: Harcourt, Brace, 1951.

Aron, Raymond, *The Opium of the Intellectuals*. New York: Norton, 1962; Paris: Calmann Lévy, 1957.

Ascherson, Neal, *The Independent*, London, January 31, 1993.

Ash, Timothy Garton, "Eastern Europe: Après le Deluge, Nous," *The New York Review of Books*, August 16, 1990.

Bailey, George, *Germans: Biography of an Obsession*. New York: World, 1972.

Barker, Ernest, "Empire," *The Encyclopaedia Britannica* (11th edition). New York: Encyclopaedia Britannica, 1911.

Béhar, Pierre, *L'Autriche-Hongrie, idée d'avenir: Permanences géopolitiques de l'Europe centrale et Balkanique*. Paris: Desjonquères, 1991.

Bell, Daniel, "Ethnicity and Social Change," in Nathan Glazer and Daniel P. Moynihan, eds., *Ethnicity: Theory and Experience*. Cambridge, Mass.: Harvard University Press, 1975.

Bell, Millicent, *Meaning in Henry James*. Cambridge, Mass.: Harvard University Press, 1991.

Berlin, Isaiah, *The Crooked Timber of Humanity: Chapters in the History of Ideas* (Henry Hardy, ed.). New York: Knopf, 1991.

———, quoted in Gardels, "Two Concepts of Nationalism," q.v.

———, quoted in O'Brien, "Paradise Lost," q.v.

Bonanno, Joe, quoted in Miller, "Agro's Aggro," q.v.

Borsody, Stephen, ed., *The Hungarians: A Divided Nation*. New Haven: Yale Center for International and Area Studies, 1988.

Butterfield, Herbert, *The Whig Interpretation of History*. London: Bell, 1931.

Cabot, George, quoted in Adams, *History of the United States During the Administrations of Thomas Jefferson*, q.v.

Carew-Hunt, R. W., *The Theory and Practice of Communism*. Baltimore: Pelican, 1963.

Carnegie, Andrew, quoted in Thompson, *Political Realism and the Crisis of World Politics*, q.v.

Coetzee, J. M., *The New York Review of Books*, January 14, 1993.

Confino, Michael, "Solzhenitsyn, the West, and the New Russian Nationalism," *The Journal of Contemporary History*, London, vol. 26/3–4, September 1991.

Craig, Gordon A., *The Germans*. New York: Meridian, 1982.

Davidson, Basil, *The Black Man's Burden: Africa and the Curse of the*

Nation-State. New York: Times Books, 1992.   241

Davis, Jefferson, quoted in Foote, *The Civil War* (vol. 1), q.v.

de Gaulle, Charles, *Doctrine politique: Recueil de déclarations et textes authentiques* (André Astoux and Guy Sabatier, eds.). Paris: Rocher, 1992.

Delors, Jacques, in the 1991 Alastair Buchan Memorial Lecture, International Institute for Strategic Studies, London.

Delperrié de Bayac, J., *Histoire de la Milice.* Paris: Fayard, 1969.

Eksteins, Modris, *Rites of Spring: The Great War and the Birth of the Modern Age.* London: Bantam, 1989.

Fitzgerald, F. Scott, *The Crack-up* (Edmund Wilson, ed.). New York: New Directions, 1945.

FitzGerald, Frances, "The American Millennium," in Sanford J. Ungar, ed., *Estrangement: America and the World.* New York: Oxford, 1985.

Foote, Shelby, *The Civil War: A Narrative* (3 vols.). New York: Random House, 1958, 1963, 1974.

Freud, Sigmund, quoted in Daniel Bell, "Ethnicity and Social Change," q.v.

Fromkin, David, *A Peace to End All Peace: The Fall of the Ottoman Empire and the Creation of the Modern Middle East.* New York: Holt, 1989.

Garde, Paul, "Trois remarques sur la position française," *Le Monde,* Paris, August 18, 1992.

———, *Vie et mort de la Yougoslavie.* Paris: Fayard, 1992.

Gardels, Nathan, "Two Concepts of Nationalism: An Interview with Isaiah Berlin," *The New York Review of Books,* November 21, 1991.

Gellner, Ernest, *Nations and Nationalism.* Oxford: Basil Blackwell, 1983.

Gibbon, Edward, *The Decline and Fall of the Roman Empire.* London: Penguin Classics, 1985.

Goldman, Eric F., *Rendezvous with Destiny: A History of Modern American Reform.* New York: Vintage, 1956.

Green, Julian, "Autobiographie," in *Oeuvres complètes.* Paris: Gallimard, Bibliothèque de la Pléiade, 1977.

Greenfeld, Liah, *Nationalism: Five Roads to Modernity.* Cambridge, Mass.: Harvard University Press, 1992.

Grundy, Congressman Felix, quoted in Adams, *History of the United States of America During the Administrations of James Madison,* q.v.

Hardwick, Elizabeth, "Mary McCarthy in New York," *The New York Review of Books,* March 26, 1992.

242   Hayes, Carlton J. H., *Nationalism: A Religion*. New York: Macmillan, 1960. (See also John Rossi, "Christianity's Great Rival," *The New Oxford Review*, Berkeley, November 1990.)

Hertzberg, Arthur, "Waiting for the Messiah," *Commonweal*, New York, May 8, 1992.

Hildebrand, Klaus, *The Third Reich*. London: Allen & Unwin, 1984.

Himmelfarb, Gertrude, *Lord Acton: A Study in Conscience and Politics*. Chicago: University of Chicago Press, 1952.

Hobsbawm, E. J., *Nations and Nationalism Since 1780*. New York: Cambridge University Press, 1990.

Hodgson, Godfrey, *The Colonel: The Life and Wars of Henry Stimson, 1867–1950*. New York: Knopf, 1990.

Hoffman, Stanley, "Nations Are Nuisances," *The New York Times Book Review*, October 7, 1990.

Hofstadter, Richard, *The American Political Tradition*. New York: Knopf, 1948.

Hook, Sidney, *Marx and the Marxists: The Ambiguous Legacy*. New York: Van Nostrand, 1955.

Hourani, Albert, *A History of the Arab Peoples*. London: Faber, 1991.

Hudson, G. F., *Europe and China: A Survey of Their Relations from the Earliest Times to 1800*. London: Edward Arnold, 1931; Boston: Beacon, 1961.

James, Henry, in a letter to Charles Eliot Norton, quoted in Millicent Bell, *Meaning in Henry James*, q.v.

Jefferson, Thomas, *Public and Private Papers*. New York: Vintage/ The Library of America, 1990.

Karaulac, Miroslav, *Libération*, Paris, March 18, 1993.

Kennan, George F., *American Diplomacy 1900–1950*. Chicago: University of Chicago Press, 1951.

———, *Around the Cragged Hill: A Personal and Political Philosophy*. New York: Norton, 1993.

Koestler, Arthur, *Arrival and Departure*. New York: Macmillan, 1943.

Lanternari, Vittorio, *The Religions of the Oppressed: A Study of Modern Messianic Cults*. New York: Knopf, 1963.

Lendvai, Paul, *Anti-Semitism in Eastern Europe*. London: Macdonald, 1972.

———, *Eagles in Cobwebs: Nationalism and Communism in the Balkans*. New York: Doubleday, 1969.

Lewis, Bernard, "In Search of Islam's Past," *The New York Review of Books*, December 5, 1991.

———, "Muslims, Christians, and Jews: The Dream of Coexistence," *The New York Review of Books*, March 26, 1992.

————, *The Political Language of Islam*. Chicago: University of   **243**
Chicago Press, 1988.

Lichtheim, George, *Imperialism*. New York: Praeger, 1971.

Lincoln, Abraham, quoted in Foote, *The Civil War* (vol. 1), q.v.

Lukacs, John, *Budapest 1900: A Historical Portrait of a City and Its Culture*. New York: Weidenfeld & Nicholson, 1988.

————, *The End of the Twentieth Century and the End of the Modern Age*. New York: Ticknor & Fields, 1993.

————, *Outgrowing Democracy: A History of the United States in the Twentieth Century*. New York: Doubleday, 1984.

Mahan, Captain Alfred Thayer, *The Influence of Sea Power upon History 1660–1783*. New York: Sagamore Press, 1957 (first published, 1890).

Mangold, Tom, *Cold Warrior: James Jesus Angleton: The CIA's Master Spy Hunter*. New York: Simon & Schuster, 1991.

Marx, Karl, *Critique of Political Economy*, quoted in Hook, *Marx and the Marxists*, q.v.

Mastny, Vojtech, and Jan Zielonka, eds., *Human Rights and Security: Europe on the Eve of a New Era*. Boulder, Colo.: Westview, 1991.

McCarthy, Mary, quoted in Hardwick, "Mary McCarthy in New York," q.v.

McKinley, William, quoted in Morgenthau, *American Foreign Policy*, q.v.

McPherson, James M., quoted in Lukacs, *The End of the Twentieth Century and the End of the Modern Age*, q.v.

Meinecke, Friedrich, quoted in Eksteins, *Rites of Spring*, q.v.

Melman, Billie, "Claiming the Nation's Past: The Invention of an Anglo-Saxon Tradition," *Journal of Contemporary History*, London, vol. 26/3–4, September 1991.

Mendoza, Juan Gonsalez de, quoted in Hudson, *Europe and China*, q.v.

Michnik, Adam, *Le Monde*, Paris, March 11, 1993.

Military Balance 1992–1993, The. London: International Institute for Strategic Studies, 1992.

Miller, Karl, "Agro's Aggro," *London Review of Books*, October 10, 1991.

Milosz, Czeslaw, quoted in Ash, "Eastern Europe," q.v.

Mirsky, Jonathan, "Squaring the Chinese Circle," *The New York Review of Books*, November 5, 1992.

Mitford, Nancy, "The English Aristocracy," *Encounter*, London, September 1955.

Morin, Edgar, "Le surgissement du total-nationalisme," *Le Monde*, Paris, March 11, 1993.

244   Monnet, Jean, *Memoirs*. New York: Doubleday, 1978.

Morgan, David, *The Mongols*. Oxford: Basil Blackwell, 1986.

Morgenthau, Hans J., *American Foreign Policy: A Critical Examination*. London: Methuen, 1952.

Morris, Richard B., and Henry Steele Commager, eds., *Encyclopedia of American History*. New York: Harper & Row, 1953.

Mosley, Sir Oswald, *My Life*. New Rochelle, N.Y.: Arlington House, 1972.

Moynihan, Daniel Patrick, *Pandaemonium: Ethnicity in International Politics*. New York: Oxford University Press, 1993.

Murray, Oswyn, "The Supremacy of Scepticism" (review of Anthony Grafton's *Defenders of the Text*), *Times Literary Supplement*, London, August 16, 1991.

Nairn, Tom, *The Break-up of Britain*. London: New Left Books, 1977.

O'Brien, Conor Cruise, "Nationalists and Democrats," *The New York Review of Books*, August 15, 1991.

———, "Paradise Lost," *The New York Review of Books*, April 25, 1991.

Okey, Robin, *Eastern Europe 1740–1985* (2d edition). London: HarperCollins, 1986.

Osgood, Herbert Levi, "United States," *The Encyclopaedia Britannica* (11th edition). New York: Encyclopaedia Britannica, 1911.

Panikkar, K. M., *Asia and Western Dominance: A Survey of the Vasco da Gama Epoch of Asian History, 1498–1945* (new edition). London: George Allen & Unwin, 1961.

Paxton, Robert O., *Vichy France: Old Guard and New Order 1940–1944*. New York: Columbia University Press, 1972.

Pfaff, William, *Barbarian Sentiments: How the American Century Ends*. New York: Hill & Wang, 1989.

———, "Getting Ahead of the Curve," *The New Yorker*, December 22, 1980.

———, "Invitation to War," *Foreign Affairs*, Summer 1993.

———, "Where the Wars Come From," *The New Yorker*, December 26, 1988.

Peissel, Michel, *The Ants' Gold*. London: Collins-Harvill, 1986.

Plesu, Andrei, interview in *Libération*, Paris, March 16, 1992.

Pomian, Krzysztof, "Une vieille fracture menace le continent," *Libération*, Paris, January 10, 1992.

Pye, Lucien, in Jonathan Mirsky, "Squaring the Chinese Circle," q.v.

Renan, Ernest, *Qu'est-ce qu'une nation? et autres essais politiques* (Joël Roman, ed.). Paris: Presses Pocket, 1992.

Ricci, Matteo, quoted in Hudson, *Europe and China*, q.v.   **245**

Rieff, David, "Seeing, Not Seeing," *Salmagundi*, Saratoga Springs, N.Y., no. 96, Fall 1992.

Roosevelt, Theodore, quoted in Hofstadter, *The American Political Tradition*, q.v.

Root, Elihu, quoted in Hodgson, *The Colonel*, q.v.

Roth, Joseph, *Hotel Savoy*. New York, 1924.

Sauzay, Brigitte, *Le vertige allemand*. Paris: Orban, 1985.

Schumpeter, Joseph, *Imperialism*. New York: Meridian, 1955.

Semprun, Jorge, *Les nouveaux cahiers*, Paris, no. 107, Winter 1991–1992.

Seton-Watson, Hugh, *Nations and States: An Inquiry into the Origins of Nations and the Politics of Nationalism*. London: Methuen, 1977.

———, "Unsatisfied Nationalisms," *The Journal of Contemporary History*, London, vol. 6/1, January 1971.

The Statesman's Year-Book, John Paxton, ed. London: Macmillan, annual.

Steel, Ronald, *Walter Lippmann and the American Century*. Boston: Little, Brown, 1980.

Stillman, Edmund, and William Pfaff, *The Politics of Hysteria: The Sources of Twentieth-Century Conflict*. New York: Harper & Row, 1964; London: Gollancz, 1964.

Stone, Norman, *Hitler*. London: Hodder & Stoughton, 1980.

Stürmer, Michael, "L'Allemagne, une question de définition," *Le Monde*, Paris, November 15–16, 1992.

Szporluk, Roman, *Communism and Nationalism: Karl Marx Versus Friedrich List*. New York: Oxford University Press, 1988.

Talmon, J. L., *Romanticism and Revolt: Europe 1815–1848*. London: Thames and Hudson, 1967.

Tawney, R. H., *Religion and the Rise of Capitalism*. London, 1926.

Taylor, A. J. P., *Europe: Grandeur and Decline*. London: Hamish Hamilton, 1950.

———, *The Hapsburg Monarchy 1809–1918*. London: Hamish Hamilton, 1948.

Thompson, Kenneth W., *Political Realism and the Crisis of World Politics: An American Approach to Foreign Policy*. Princeton: Princeton University Press, 1960.

Tocqueville, Alexis de, *Democracy in America* (the Henry Reeve text as revised, 2 vols.; Phillips Bradley, ed.). New York: Vintage, 1954.

———, *The European Revolution and Correspondence with Gobineau* (John Lukacs, ed. and transl.). New York: Anchor, 1959.

246   Toynbee, Arnold, *A Study of History* (abridgment of vols. I–VI by D. C. Somervell). New York: Oxford University Press, 1946.

Trotsky, Leon, "La révolution étranglée" (a critique of André Malraux's *The Conquerors*), *La nouvelle revue française*, no. 211, April 1, 1931; reprinted in the Pléiade *Oeuvres complètes* of Malraux (vol. 1). Paris: Gallimard, 1989.

Turner, Frederick Jackson, "United States," *The Encyclopaedia Britannica* (11th edition). New York: Encyclopaedia Britannica, 1911.

Turner, Henry A., "It's Time to Scrap the Myth of the German 'Volk,' " *The International Herald Tribune*, Paris, December 22, 1992.

Vidal, Gore, "Lincoln Up Close," *The New York Review of Books*, August 15, 1991.

Volkan, Vamik D., and Norman Itzkowitz, *The Immortal Atatürk: A Psychobiography*. Chicago: University of Chicago Press, 1984.

Wittfogel, Karl A., *Oriental Despotism: A Comparative Study of Total Power*. New Haven: Yale University Press, 1957.

Wolff, Leon, *Little Brown Brother*. New York: Longmans, 1960.

Wood, Gordon S., "Americans and Revolutionaries," *The New York Review of Books*, September 27, 1990.

Woodruff, Philip, *The Guardians*. New York: St. Martin's, 1954.

Woolf, S. J., ed., *European Fascism*. New York: Vintage, 1969.

Zamoyski, Adam, *The Polish Way: A Thousand-Year History of the Poles and Their Culture*. London: John Murray, 1987.

Index

About the Author

William Pfaff's most recent book, *Barbarian Sentiments*, was a National Book Award finalist, and in French translation won the City of Geneva's Prix Jean-Jacques Rousseau as the best political work of 1989–1990.

His reflections on politics and contemporary history have appeared in *The New Yorker* since 1971. He writes a column for *The International Herald Tribune* in Paris, syndicated by the *Los Angeles Times*.

He is the former deputy director of the Hudson Institute's European affiliate, and before that was an officer of the Free Europe organization. He is a former editor of *Commonweal* magazine. He was born in Iowa, spent his adolescence in Georgia, and is a graduate of the University of Notre Dame.